Testimonials

As an interpreter I have seen too many patients and their husbands struggle with cancer. This book provides perfect guidance for people in this situation.
Chiuming

This book will help every man faced with the seemingly insurmountable challenge of caring for a wife with cancer. Written from a place of deep reflection following personal experience, James provides heartfelt and inspiring encouragement to blokes in a similar situation. This is a must-have book to accompany you or a loved one at whatever stage of the journey they are on.
Oliver Giudici

We may not yet have a cure for cancer, but this book is the magic pill men need to help them navigate their emotions and roles during this unknown journey. So many powerful tools in one place! A must!
Adrian Addamo

This book is certainly honest. But it is a lot more than that: it is courageous, knowledgeable, practical and wise. Read it and learn!
D. Dizdar, prior of the Emmaus monastic community

As James' brother I witnessed first-hand how difficult this journey was for him as Natasha's husband. I didn't realise just how hard it was until I saw it, and this is likely the case for you – silently going

about your massive job with very few people stopping to ask how you're going or even aware of your unique needs. Most men I find like to have answers quickly and easily accessible, and this book gives you that. Dealing with a cancer diagnosis and ongoing treatments of your main support and love will cloud every judgement you make and help with this won't come easily. The more support and information you have the easier it is for everyone.
Tristan Gutteridge

Dealing with tragedy will never be easy, but this inspiring story provides real, practical advice to help you get through it.
James Centenera

A highly practical and thoughtful guidebook based largely on lived experience. Caregiving just got easier
Jan Saggers

Gutteridge's book is like having a life coach beside you every step of this difficult journey. No man would wish to be faced with James' tragic circumstances (and there are many who are!) but those men who do will find this book a great boon. James has taken his own tragedy and suffering and transformed it into a guide for men who suddenly find themselves caring for their partner diagnosed with cancer. James' book will act as a first responder, mentor and friend to those men who are feeling overwhelmed, alone and bewildered, faced with probably their biggest challenge in life. James' book will give invaluable assistance to men who unexpectedly become carers for their wives diagnosed with cancer. A strong message underlies the book which challenges popular notions of masculinity: Men too have a great capacity to care - they just might need a little nudge and a few tips to do it well!
James Wishart

SO YOUR WIFE HAS CANCER

JAMES GUTTERIDGE

SO YOUR WIFE HAS CANCER

THE MAN'S ULTIMATE GUIDE
FOR HOW TO COPE AND WHAT TO DO

INSPIRED
PUBLISHING

So Your Wife Has Cancer
The Man's Ultimate Guide For How To Cope and What To Do
First Edition, First Impression 2021
ISBN 978-1-77630-672-5
Copyright © James Gutteridge

Published by:
Inspired Publishing
PO Box 82058 I Southdale I 2135
Johannesburg , South Africa
Email: info@inspiredpublishing.co.za
www.inspiredpublishing.co.za

TABLE OF CONTENTS

Dedication

This is for all husbands and their wives who are facing this immense journey together.

In Loving Memory of Natasha
1986 – 2017

Disclaimer

The author of this book does not dispense medical advice or other related professional advice. He does not prescribe the use of any technique as a form of diagnosis or treatment for any physical, emotional or medical condition. The intent of the author is only to offer information of an anecdotal and general nature that may be part of the reader's quest for emotional and physical well-being.

In the event the reader or others use any of the information or other content in this book, the author and the publisher assume no responsibility for the direct or indirect consequences. The reader should consult his or her medical, health, or related professional before adopting any of the advice in this book or drawing inferences from it.

If You Only Read This: My Top Five Pieces of Advice

This book covers every aspect of caring for yourself and your wife but here are my top five pieces of advice, knowing that your time can be short. Treat this like a cheat sheet you come back to in times of emergency or for a refresher.

1. If In Personal Crisis, See A Doctor And/Or Call A Helpline

Before we go any further, if you are in a personal crisis at the time of reading this see a doctor immediately. If this is not possible right now, then call a helpline. These services help with mental health support, suicide-prevention services and emotional assistance. You can search for 'lifeline' in your country, and there is a Wikipedia page entitled 'List of suicide crisis lines' which gives you options globally.

As you'll read in the book, I found myself in severe crisis mode soon after my wife Natasha was diagnosed - depressed and unable to get out of bed - and even thinking suicidal thoughts. I didn't go to a doctor because I thought I could deal with the depression on my own, so I spent the next year struggling to climb out of a dark hole just to function. I couldn't give my full attention to Natasha. I'd never had mental health issues before and had never seen a doctor about it, so I didn't even know I could go to them for help.

Once I did, though, I wish I had been told sooner that this was an option. The doctor prescribed me antidepressants and told me to see a psychologist. Both were crucial to me becoming a champion carer and husband for Natasha. I got off the medication gradually once the immediate crisis was over.

Seriously, if you're not feeling 100% right now put down this book and either see a general practitioner /family doctor (I'll refer to these doctors as a GP throughout the book), or call a helpline, or both.

2. You Cannot Care For Your Wife If You Do Not Look After Yourself

You'll probably feel selfish when caring for yourself, but not only is self-care self*less* - it's vital. Your emotional, mental and physical well-being are crucial for your success as a champion carer and husband because your wife's energy will often be running low. This new role will take more out of you than you could imagine, so take time for yourself and communicate your needs and feelings with your wife, your closest family and friends, as well as with doctors.

3. You Are A Carer Now. This Is Your New Mission And Purpose

Most partners in this situation don't identify as carers. They might think a carer is someone in an official role, like a nurse, or in a role that isn't unexpected, like a child who is caring for an elderly parent. The sooner you come to terms with the fact that you're a carer, *as well as* a husband, the easier this will be. Accepting this as your role helps you approach the situation differently and alter your expectations.

This doesn't mean you'll instantly be a great carer. In fact it's guaranteed that you'll make mistakes, some quite drastic ones. Don't berate yourself for these as they are an inevitable and necessary step towards learning how to become a world-class carer, just as Einstein was born unable to do mathematics and science yet learned and became a genius.

4. You Are Never Alone. Extensive Research Has Shown That All Partners In Your Situation Suffer Enormously

Even your wildest feelings - like being helpless, wanting to leave the situation, or being angry with your wife - are normal. Recognise your feelings and have the courage not to act on them impulsively. Take the time to sit with them, meditate on them, and discuss them. Therapists and doctors, even if you see your wife's doctor, are sworn to confidentiality.

Focus on what you *can* still control, even if it's only one small part of your day. This book will show you that there is much you can actually control even if everything feels out of control.

5. You Will Grow From This In Ways Beyond Your Imagination

Perhaps the most unforeseen aspect of this journey is the tremendous growth you'll experience as a husband, carer, employee, or in whatever you do in life. Have hope that no matter what happens, everything you learn throughout this extreme trial will make you truly bulletproof to life's other inevitable challenges.

Foreword

Patrick O'Sullivan

I received an early draft of *So Your Wife Has Cancer* after James sent a copy to friends, asking for feedback. I'm not much of a reader generally and had no experience with cancer or support, so I left it for our other (smarter) friends to read and help James. Neither of us knew it yet, but one day I would be frantically searching through two-year old emails to find that book so I'd have a clue of what to do.

My fiancée had called to tell me she'd be home late. She had to wait in the city for a second procedure her dermatologist had insisted she stay back for. The doctor thought it would be best to remove a suspicious mole on the same day. I was relieved – if it was cancer, it was gone. A week later, we got the results. It was melanoma and more developed than her dermatologist had anticipated. My fiancée required a procedure where more tissue would be removed around the original location of the melanoma and a lymph-node test would be conducted to check if little cells of cancer had broken free and collected there. Big news. We were scared. Then, we received a second call – she had been exposed to a known case of COVID-19. She was legally required to isolate for 14 days until Easter. This meant she could not have this potentially life-saving treatment for at least three weeks.

I was terrified. I couldn't help but think of those little cancer cells breaking free and travelling around her body and forming little footholds. I didn't know what to do, so I dug out James' old email and started reading his book. It wasn't easy. James' story was tough. I'd seen it in person and was horrified that the same might be happening to me.

But I knew that tough news is best delivered straight. I know James and that he always finds ways of making the best of a bad situation. This book frames cancer as a journey we go on together, one where our relationship could become stronger. Even if this wasn't a journey either of us wanted to go on.

This book focuses on the importance of the mental health of the caregiver which - notably for me - had already begun to deteriorate, even though we were only early on in the journey. It is also a tome of practical advice with many tips I would never even have considered.

I attended the next appointment with my fiancée when the surgeon told us the lymph-node test had come back positive and contained a small number of melanoma cells. It had spread. My vision narrowed and I felt light-headed. Had I heard it right? But my fiancée's eyes confirmed it. I had called James earlier in the week to ask for his help, but nothing really prepares you for news like this. I didn't even want to respond to James' messages asking me how the results had gone. But I took James' advice to book an appointment with my GP to focus on my own mental health. It was becoming clear I was not going to be the carer I needed to be unless I cared for myself.

James has described the book to me as one he wished he had had at the start of his journey, a kind of guide or manual to help a carer know what to do. This is exactly how I thought of the book, even skipping ahead to sections that covered topics I was particularly worried about. There are concepts that may or may not resonate with you because this is a book for men of all walks of life. Take on board what works for you. The book is filled with gems that will make your journey easier. Some of them will be obvious to different people - for example, I wasn't sure if I should ask to attend my partner's appointments - and others are more complicated.

James' journey was long and very difficult. I am glad he has taken the time to impart his valuable advice to many others. My partner is now cancer-free so our journey is done. Your journey will be different, hopefully shorter than both of ours, but if it isn't then this book should be one of the first things you read after you find out your wife has cancer.

All the best in your journey.
Pat

Introduction

"Contrary to the myth, nurturing isn't an innate default setting in the human female. It is active and requires strength, stamina, will, intelligence, and determination: all of the qualities that we tend to associate with maleness."
- Christiane Northrup MD, Mother Daughter Wisdom

Dear Champion Husband,

First, you'll hear this often but not always from people who understand your situation: I'm deeply sorry your wife has cancer. There is no sugar-coating how screwed up this news is.

Shortly after my wife Natasha was diagnosed in June 2014, I found myself alone in a hotel room next to Sydney airport when a plane flew overhead. Natasha and I were meant to be on that plane. We had planned a holiday to Vancouver, but instead I was now about to board a plane to Manila, capital of the Philippines. Natasha was already there, having travelled a week earlier for her grandmother's funeral. A couple of days after the funeral, Natasha had a colonoscopy and was strongly suspected of having cancer. Now, instead of us going to Vancouver, I was sitting in the hotel scared, bewildered, in shock and disbelief, and without the faintest idea of what to do next. How could this be happening? Surely cancer happens to other people and not us? I can empathise with your situation and am truly sorry you are in it.

Second, I'm extremely happy you're reading this book, even though ideally you would never need to read it. When Natasha was diagnosed, I said jokingly to my friends, "Wouldn't it be great if there was a guide for what to do when your wife gets cancer?" Jokes always have an element of truth in them, though, and I desperately needed that guide. It never came, so after Natasha died nearly four years later I decided to write it myself.

This book you hold now is that guide and, having gone through what you're now facing, I hope you're able to learn from all my mistakes – some of them were quite big ones! I had zero idea how to be a great carer and husband in this situation and had to learn everything the hard way, through trial and error, with plenty of error. After Natasha died I found dozens of scientific papers researching the carer's journey and that research has further informed this book. As I digested the research, I was frustrated. Why was there no guide to help carers when there was so much research showing how difficult the journey is for them? I talked to oncologists about the research and discovered it was never even taught to them.

As I wrote this guide, using that research and my experience, I imagined myself sitting with you, sharing stories, lessons, advice, and heartache, just like I've already had to do with friends. I'm walking with you through this book, helping you along, one man to another. You can come back to these words anytime you need hope, encouragement and advice.

The problems facing male partner carers are unique, so a book needs to be tailored specifically to men. When I first talked to people about the idea for this book, they asked, "Why are you only writing for husbands? Why not for wives with husbands who have cancer? Or for men who are carers of disabled children or elderly parents?" I've wrestled with these questions. The main reason is that husband cancer carers have particular needs, and there are no books out there aimed specifically at men. There is a clear gender difference between the outcomes for men and women carers. Research shows that women cope better than men in this situation. Women are generally better at building support networks to reach out to. They find it easier to understand and express emotions to their support network.

We've been raised in a society that tells us men to be strong for our wives and families, and that hiding emotion shows strength. We're told there's something wrong if we cannot deal with challenges on our own without help. But that's only a belief and we can choose to believe whatever we want to. Believing in outdated ideas that don't work is not the choice we will make. Finally, there are specific issues partner-carers face that are irrelevant for other carers, such as managing a romantic relationship. The proximity they have to the patient causes unique complications.

Men also respond to different language and you will notice I use the words 'Hero' and 'Champion' quite a lot. Of course, you might not feel like either of those things at the moment, but this book is about helping you become a champion carer and realising that in many ways you already are.

As to the book being only for cancer carers, cancer is a unique disease in that people are now living with it for longer, which brings incredible uncertainty. Cancer has unique treatment options compared to other chronic illnesses.

No two men, or two couples, are the same. Whatever your situation is, my sincere hope is that this book helps you in some way, especially in giving you the confidence that you can do this. My hope for you, and the overarching reason I wrote this book, is for you to grow to become a heroic carer, husband, and man. The journey will shape you in ways you could never imagine. This book can be your guide in approaching the journey with confidence, love, strength, optimism, resilience, help from others, humility and grit.

Finally, a note for male partners in a de facto relationship, partners who identify as male and partners in a same-sex relationship: this book is for you as well. I have written with an explicitly masculine tone as it's distinct from the feminine. The needs of male partners are unique, but if you're a man with a partner, this book is for you. LGBTQI couples dealing with cancer have further unique difficulties and, while this area is not my area of expertise, I'm sure this book will help you and I encourage you to look up specific resources to accompany it. I'm writing from the perspective of a male with a female wife and, for the sake of brevity, from now on I'll refer to the reader as a husband and the patient as a wife.

If just one suggestion in this book helps you and your wife, then I consider it a success. Good luck as you go through the journey.

Your friend,
James

How to Use This Book

There are eight parts to this book, each distinct and with a standalone focus. What you'll do as you go through this book is build a strategy.

The strategy won't cover every possible scenario but, in the planning process, you set yourself up with the healthiest mindset, attitude and skill-set possible.

You can prepare for most scenarios and situation changes. You're building a world-class toolkit to become a world-class carer and husband.

Part 1: So Your Wife Has Cancer
We begin by looking at what you could be feeling right now, and how you can re-frame this journey in a different, more positive way.

Part 2: Your Mindset
Parts 2 to 4 focus on caring for yourself first because you must be in the best shape you can be - mentally, emotionally and physically - to care for your wife. Part 2 focuses on your mindset, teaching you how to build courage, control, flexibility, a growth mindset, and gratitude.

Part 3: You Are Never Alone
This is about how to care for yourself by finding help from others. It covers who could help you, how to find them, and how to ask for help.

Part 4: Caring for You
Here the guide covers the practical tools to help you care for yourself, such as diet, sleep and powerful habits.

Part 5: Your Wife's Treatment
In Part 5 you'll learn all about your wife's treatment, interacting with her doctors, planning techniques, and tools to care for her at home.

Part 6: Caring For Each Other
Here topics such as communication, sex, intimacy and children are covered.

Part 7: End of Life
In Part 7, I help you to prepare for the end of life if the worst does eventually happen.

Part 8: The Hero is Changed Forever

Finally, you'll see how you change forever in every aspect of your life, in ways you could never expect as you have gone through this journey.

I suggest reading from the beginning all the way through, and then coming back to chapters depending on which is most relevant for the situation you find yourself in at the time. Although the book is structured to be read from beginning to end, there will be specific topics you need help with right now, so you can go straight to those.

HOW TO APPROACH THE EXERCISES IN THE BOOK

Throughout this book, I invite you to complete short exercises which will appear in boxes like this one. It's completely up to you how you do this: in your head, on paper, or electronically. The idea of writing things like this might be foreign (it was for me) but like anything, it gets easier over time.

The research on journaling clearly points to benefits. I feel like I'm downloading stuff out of my head onto paper or my electronic notebook, so I have more space in my head for other information.

I use the built-in Notes app on my phone because it syncs seamlessly with my laptop and is quick to open. I can also protect it with a passcode or fingerprint, which gives me the freedom to write whatever I want. I recommend setting up a new notebook or buying a new notebook if you want to write by hand, specifically for cancer. You could call it 'Cancer Notebook'.

Then you can create individual notes corresponding to each exercise. If you want to write your notebook by hand, but don't yet have a notebook, write in these book margins if you're reading the paperback. Use the notes function on your e-book reader, write on some paper or on your computer, phone for now. If you don't even have those handy, take the time to just reflect on the exercises in your head. Aiming for perfection is the enemy of doing what is good enough.

PART ONE

SO YOUR WIFE HAS CANCER

We begin by looking at what you're likely feeling right now, and how you can re-frame this journey in a different, more positive way.

1.1

The Diagnosis Reaction
And How Your Grief
Has Already Begun

Let's start from the beginning, even if you're picking up this book long after your wife has been diagnosed.

We begin with the exercise on the next page.

EXERCISE: DIAGNOSTIC REACTION

Write down your immediate reactions to, or emotions from, hearing about the diagnosis in a note titled Diagnosis Reaction, or take a moment to think about it instead of writing. If you're past the diagnosis stage as you read this, write down what you're feeling right now and title your note accordingly. Your reactions are probably a mixture of:

- Anger;
- Wanting to hit something;
- No idea what to do;
- Not having an idea of how you are going to cope;
- Disbelief;
- Actual disbelief/doubt that this is happening;
- Still in shock;
- Overwhelmed by it all;
- Feeling sick;
- Feeling exhausted;
- Headache;
- Anger towards your wife;
- Alone;
- No feelings at all.

Don't worry if you find this difficult. Maybe you only have one reaction, which might be 'no feelings at all'. My instinct has always been to think rather than feel. When Natasha first called me from the Philippines to tell me about her colonoscopy results, the news didn't sink in for a long time. Two years after Natasha's diagnosis, when I was seeing a psychologist, they asked me, "What are you feeling?" I had no idea how to respond. The cancer didn't feel real and I carried on living with zero emotional reaction. Though I didn't register it in my mind, my body was keeping the score with a higher blood pressure, shorter temper and increased alcohol consumption. My mind went into survival mode because I had so much to get done. I was in problem-solving mode, not feeling mode, which you might be in too.

It's important not to judge yourself for any of the feelings, or lack of them, you have right now. You and your feelings are unique, because often they are tied up with beliefs and feelings we have formed since childhood.

RIGHT FROM DIAGNOSIS, YOUR GRIEF HAS ALREADY BEGUN

Many people believe that we only grieve when somebody passes away. This isn't the case: humans grieve all the time. To grieve means to feel intense sorrow, to mourn, or to be distressed. Its origins are from the old French word *grever*, which means burden, and the Latin word *gravis*, which means heavy or serious. To feel grief means to feel burdened about something serious, which could be anything.

We instinctively know this by the language society uses. For example, difficult people can cause us grief. There is plenty in life that can cause us grief: the loss of a job, financial hardship, moving to a new city, or dealing with a difficult colleague. Whatever it is, the feeling of grief is associated with any life difficulty.

Without having consciously realised it, you're probably grieving following your wife's diagnosis. Some researchers refer to this as premature or anticipatory grief due to anticipating the death and the loss of someone. This isn't necessarily the case. The grief is real and directly related to what you're experiencing right now because you might not be anticipating anything.

Grief makes sense when you think about some of the possible changes in your life due to the cancer diagnosis:

- Seeing your wife experience a full range of emotional challenges;
- Trying to understand what cancer is;
- Upset to your daily routines;
- Questions you are now answering from those around you;
- Reduction in income if your wife was working, or if you need to reduce your hours;
- Freedom to travel wherever you wanted, whenever you wanted, without worrying about doctor appointments and energy levels;
- Change in your relationship's intimacy;
- Time you could spend with your mates that you now spend caring;
- Your emotions used to be in control, now nothing is certain;
- Your future used to be somewhat predictable but now it's not.

EXERCISE: THE CHANGES

Write down the biggest changes in your life caused by the cancer diagnosis. It's useful to see these changes written down in order to acknowledge that these changes are real and not just in your imagination. If you don't feel like writing, just take a few moments to reflect instead.

It's clear your whole life has changed, which means you'll naturally be grieving due to the heaviness and burden of this.

Why does it matter that you're already grieving? You'll understand that grief is probably what is causing these confusing changes or reactions that you're possibly feeling. It's not that you're coping poorly. It's a natural part of being human to grieve what you've lost and what has changed in your life. You can be easier on yourself knowing this grief and the feelings that come with it are normal. Grief is like nothing else you'll experience. It's an entire range of emotions flooding your mind or being experienced in your body that are often uncontrollable and can be intense.

GRIEF: NOT A LINEAR PROGRESSION THROUGH FIVE CLEAN STAGES

You may have heard of there being five stages of grief. Describing grief as stages can be problematic, though, because people might think they progress through each stage consecutively. Or they might think they are done with a stage, so that stage won't come back. This is not true. You could experience any of the stages at any time in any order, and sometimes all at once, which is overwhelming. If you're feeling exhausted or on the verge of burnout right now, grief is probably a large part of the reason why. I find it easier to think of grief as having components instead of stages. Those components include:

Denial
Denial is a protective mechanism that is hard-wired into us. Our minds are designed to numb the shock of our emotions so we can still function. If my mind hadn't kicked into numbing the shock, I would have been a complete mess and in no way able to help Natasha. If anyone questions your apparent numbness and ambivalence to the situation, know you're not a heartless bastard and this is a normal part of the grieving process. You can look at this denial component with gratitude as it's an impressive mind mechanism to help you cope and help you help your wife.

Anger

You know what anger is. People feel it all the time. Nobody will blame you for being angry at seeing your wife in pain and your life being turned upside down. I'll discuss this in more detail throughout the book.

Bargaining

In the bargaining component of grief, all you want is to return to how life was before. You might look at the list above, of everything that has changed for you, and would do anything to be back to 'normal'. This was most true for me when seeing Natasha in immense pain, and I would have literally done anything to get rid of that pain. Unfortunately, there's no bargain you can make to return to normal, so dealing with this perceived lack of control will be covered in Part 2.

Depression

There's a lot of talk these days about depression. But if you haven't experienced depression before, you might assume - like I did before it happened to me - that it's just a feeling of sadness that can simply be snapped out of. This isn't the case so we'll discuss depression and how to deal with it in plenty of detail throughout the book.

Acceptance

You will eventually accept what has happened, which may be hard to believe and hopefully reassuring. One of the goals of this book is to help you accept what you cannot control, and I'll give you some tools to help you do this. Be reassured, though, that even if you come to accept the situation, emotions like anger and depression may still arise.

Acceptance is a process, and some days it's easier than others. I found that how well I accepted the cancer depended on how well Natasha was at the time. If she was smiling and had a bit of energy to go for a meal or a short trip, I felt like maybe we were all right. Then other days, when I would see her unable to get out of bed, I found the cancer hard to accept and became angry, albeit silently. Grief is not a linear progression though five clean stages.

EXERCISE: YOUR GRIEF STAGE

Which components of grief are you in right now? Write this down, if you feel like it. There is no need to justify it as you are the only one reading this.

I will talk more about grief throughout this book and in Part 7 I will look at a method to process your grief systematically.

You may be feeling one or all of these aspects of grief, sometimes all at once, and sometimes in unexpected waves. There is no right or wrong reaction or emotion and it's common to feel a range of emotions at different times.

YOU ARE NOT ALONE

It's common to feel alone in this situation, like you're the only one who has had your life uprooted. The reality is there are thousands of other men like you who are becoming carers for their wives, and they may be just as confused and unprepared as you are and as I was.

In 2019, there were around 30 000 new cancer diagnoses in Australia every year for women in a married or de facto relationship (over 60 000 women, in total, were newly diagnosed). On top of this, there are around 160 000 women currently living with cancer who are married or in de facto relationships in Australia. By 2040, there will be 400 000 married women, or women in de facto relationships, living with cancer.

Globally, these numbers are even more staggering. There are currently over three million married women, or women in de facto relationships who are diagnosed with cancer every year. This is projected to rise to about five million in 2030.

These numbers are horrifying yet can be comforting too. It's horrible that so many couples have had their lives uprooted, not to mention the couples where the husband has been diagnosed. But it's comforting to know you're not alone in this struggle. There are millions of men trying to work out what on earth happened to their life and are somehow figuring out how to be a great carer to the woman they have committed their life to. These numbers might not help with the feeling of aloneness though, and we discuss this in a whole section of the book – Part 3.

1.2

Becoming a Caregiver: Some Serious Reactions and Feelings

The previous chapter looked at how drastically your whole life as a couple has changed, and some of the feelings you have at the moment. The purpose of this chapter is to go deeper with those feelings, the idea of wanting to leave, and the concept of indefinite loss.

STAY OR LEAVE

At some point you may have thoughts of leaving your wife. This may come with a sense of guilt but rest assured: it's normal. Your life has been thrown upside down. The same dreams you once had have been put on hold, and that nagging loss of control is always there.

One of the main reasons I wrote this book was because of the statistics about how common separation and divorce are as a reaction to a wife's cancer diagnosis. Rather than ask why you would feel like doing this, instead you might ask how could you not feel like leaving? Most of us in tough situations, such as having a difficult boss, will probably try to leave that situation. Why wouldn't you have those feelings about leaving your situation? A study of 515 patients with a serious medical illness - who were married when diagnosed - found the rate of divorce when a female was the patient was six times higher (20% of marriages) than when men were the patient (about 3%).[1]

Anyone who judges someone for thinking about walking away has no idea how hard the partner carer role truly is. When I read those statistics, I could understand. Even my own family and friends had no idea how hard being a carer was until they came to visit. Some people couldn't believe I didn't just leave Natasha. I could never have left, though sometimes the thoughts were powerful and unrelenting. My mind was always convincing me to leave the Philippines, that I was not that important to her anyway because I could not fix the cancer, that I could just go back to my job and be close to my family and friends, finally get a solid night's sleep, and do what I wanted to do again.

After all, you didn't choose for your wife to have cancer and for your life to be uprooted. You may be thinking that you could just choose to leave and regain that sense of control which had been taken away from you. You could start a relationship with someone who isn't sick, you could work your normal hours again, you wouldn't have to go to hospital, and you could get rid of much of the stress in your life. Life is hard enough without dealing with your wife's cancer on top of it.

---

1 Glantz, M. et.al., Gender disparity in the rate of partner abandonment in patients with serious medical illness, Cancer, 2009, Nov 2015 5;115(22):5237-42

And as men we like to have some kind of influence. We like to fix problems. But we cannot fix cancer. So, what's the point of staying around anyway? You might think that, because there's so little you can do to help your wife, she wouldn't notice if you left. It's not like she has a scratch you can just put a bandage on. Cancer doesn't give a toss what you do; it will do what it wants to anyway.

Thoughts and actions are not the same. Try not to judge yourself too harshly for having these thoughts. Someone who thinks of killing someone, which is most of us, is different to someone who actually kills someone, which is few of us.

There is another voice in your heart that will stop you from leaving. Sometimes this voice will be difficult to hear, but it's there. You signed up for this when you married your wife, in sickness and in health. And it doesn't matter if you haven't yet married with these vows. You love her, and part of loving someone is sacrificing yourself for them.

Recognise that although it sounds nice to start a relationship with someone else who is healthy, every relationship has problems - even between healthy people. You know working normal hours and having a solid sleep sounds great, but that's not all there is to a good life.

Your wife does need you, more than you may know, even if much of the time you might not feel needed. With the help of this guide you can overcome the thoughts, feelings and situations that make you feel worthless. In the next few parts of this book you'll learn how to re-frame your purpose as your wife's champion carer, how to help your wife when you feel helpless, how to gain control when nothing seems in control, and how to re-think your relationship with your job.

Ultimately, consider making the braver choice rather than the cowardly choice: the choice to stay and fight alongside your wife, though neither of you chose to be on this journey.

INDEFINITE LOSS

Another feeling you might be having is that of indefinite loss, which is one of the hardest aspects of dealing with your wife's cancer. Indefinite loss is the unique feeling of loss that cancer carers experience. It is not connected to the loss that comes at the terminal or bereavement stage. A study of Australian caregivers (18 husbands and 14 wives) found that 26 of them, over 80%, experienced indefinite loss.[2]

Instead of focusing on the difficulty of planning for the future, carers now have to focus on what is in front of them, right here and now. But even the present is difficult to adjust to: sometimes it's impossible to know what will happen even today, let alone tonight or tomorrow. You might think about treating your wife to a nice holiday but you're not sure if she will have the energy to enjoy the holiday or if your wife's doctor will allow her to travel.

The inability to plan for the future means many carers feel trapped in time, unable to confidently move forward or return to a pre-cancer life with their spouse. You're dealing with the past, future and present all at once. On top of trying to focus on the present, and deal with an uncertain future, you're dealing with the loss of your past life together. Your life as a couple radically changed since the diagnosis. No wonder this is the hardest job you've ever

2 Olson, R.E. (2014), Indefinite loss: the experiences of carers of a spouse with cancer, European Journal of Cancer Care, 23, 553-561

had to do!

One carer interviewed in the study, Charlie, mentioned that 'the future has got down to what I am doing this afternoon almost. Never mind next week stuff.'[3]

Another carer, Rodney, felt guilty about trying to make investment decisions that could not rely on his wife's income if she was too unwell to work. He couldn't make plans without uncertainty or guilt.

In the past, a cancer diagnosis used to mean an automatic death sentence. Thanks to modern medicine, death is not always inevitable. This is great news but does little to help with the uncertain future, difficult present, and grief about a lost past that caregivers feel. This unique aspect of cancer is another reason I wrote this book.

Despite these feelings you might have, of questioning your purpose and ability to stay as well as of indefinite loss, there is a way to frame this journey that makes sense, which we explore in the next chapter.

---

3 Ibid., p. 558

1.3

The Hero's Journey

*"A hero is someone who has given his or her life
to something bigger than oneself."*
- Joseph Campbell

The Hero's Journey is a concept that connects every lesson in this guide. The fact that you're a hero on this journey with your wife possibly seems strange because, like I did, you would never consider yourself a hero. But once you understand this mythical concept, and see how it applies to this new situation, you'll come to realise how this is a core part of your whole life.

The idea of The Hero's Journey was popularised in the book The Power of Myth by mythologist and writer Joseph Campbell. The concept has been analysed extensively since then and influenced George Lucas to base the story structure of *Star Wars* on it. The best directors now refuse to produce a script if it fails to fit into this structure.

The word *hero* comes from the Greek word *heros*, which means "protector" and "defender". You are your wife's protector and defender. You've been called to safeguard her as best as you possibly can. What is the journey heroes must go on?

The simplest explanation of the hero's journey follows seven steps:
1. The hero is living an ordinary life;
2. The hero is called on an adventure they don't want to go on;
3. The hero realises they must do this quest anyway;
4. A wise mentor comes along to guide the hero through this journey;
5. The journey becomes unbearably tough with multiple challenges;
6. The hero eventually succeeds with help from others and grows unbelievably strong in the process;
7. The hero comes back to ordinary life transformed, never to be the same.

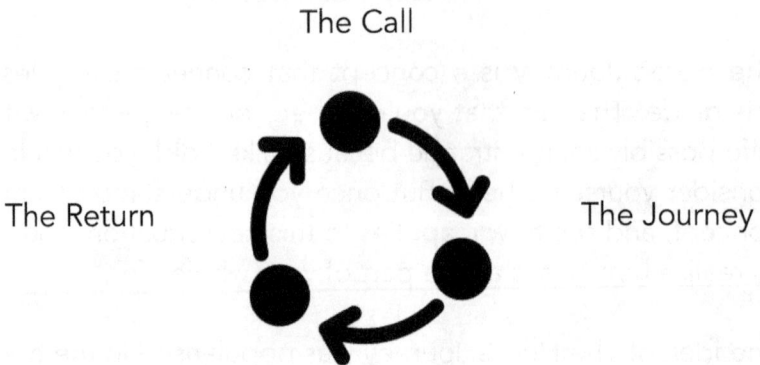

The Call

The Return
The Journey

J.R.R. Tolkien's *The Lord of the Rings* is a great example of this journey:

1. Think of Frodo the Hobbit living a comfortable and happy life in the serene, safe Shire;
2. Then Bilbo goes away, leaving the ring with Frodo. Gandalf informs Frodo that the ring needs to be destroyed in a faraway mountain, which serves as the call to this adventure or journey. But Frodo is reluctant to leave his comfort zone and refuses the call;
3. Soon Frodo realises he is the only one who can carry out the task, and there is great danger if he does not do so;
4. Gandalf mentors Frodo and guides him along the way, accompanied by other hobbits;
5. Throughout the journey Frodo is challenged through extreme trials, but overcomes them with his previously unknown powers and the help of others;
6. Ultimately, Frodo eventually succeeds in destroying the ring;
7. He then returns to the Shire, transformed in his mindset, abilities, belief in himself, and friendships.

What a story! When you think of many of your favourite stories, this is the basic format they all follow because the whole point of myths is to expose what is in our innermost minds as human beings. Frodo is a *hero* because he is a *protector* who destroys the ring and its evil powers.

EXERCISE: YOUR HERO'S JOURNEY
In a new note, entitled My Hero's Journey, which you'll come back to throughout, write down the seven steps and identify which is your current position on the journey:

The hero is living an ordinary life: You have well and truly left this life behind. Write a few words down about that life, such as comfortable, planned out, and happy.

The hero is called on an adventure that they don't want to be on: You don't want your wife to be on this journey and you would do anything to see her free of cancer. What are your feelings at this stage, e.g., scared, disbelief, shock, anger, reluctance?

The hero realises that they must go on this journey anyway: You'll be reluctant at first to go on this journey, especially with all of the changes it brings. But ultimately you are your wife's hero, and this will be starkly clear to you when you see her in physical or emotional pain for the first time. Your wife needs all the help she can get, and she has been blessed with an heroic husband to help her through this. So, you agree to go on this journey, knowing (or maybe not knowing yet) that it's going to be the absolute hardest thing you'll ever do in your life. Are you at this stage? How does it feel? Do you feel a deep sense of responsibility? Do you feel like a warrior going to battle?

A wise mentor comes along to guide the hero through this journey: Like your wife, you'll also need all the help you can get, which is where this book fits in. It will give you the mindset and skillset you require along the journey and, while I look nothing like Gandalf, think of me and this guide as a mentor. Who else can be a mentor for you?

The journey becomes unbearably tough to the point of wanting to quit: How many times have you already felt this? What struggles have you already felt? Would it just be easier to give up?

The hero eventually succeeds with help from others and grows unbelievably strong in the process: You will become your wife's ultimate heroic protector and defender. You'll be a champion carer and husband.

The hero comes back to ordinary life, completely transformed: You will never be the same. We have dedicated all of Part 8 to exploring how this happens.

The final part of the Hero's Journey can be a difficult one to understand, where the Hero returns to the life he had before. You might believe that if you protect your wife valiantly and give her the utmost care, then you've fulfilled the calling given to you. This is true, but you'll grow from facing the trials of this journey so it's inevitable you'll be transformed and then help change others. In short, anyone who can face this journey can then face anything.

Your journey will be a unique one. Whether you like it or not, you're on this journey and **you are a Hero, your wife's protector.** You've got this! You are rising up and taking on this immense challenge. You are like David facing Goliath, refusing to let Goliath (the cancer) take you down, and you'll do everything you can to be the champion carer and husband your wife needs you to be. I congratulate you and suggest that you congratulate yourself for responding to the call, for being wise enough to realise you need help - starting with this book. Now, in Part 2, let's begin to learn about the tools you have at your disposal.

KEY POINTS FROM PART 1

1. Your reaction to the diagnosis includes a range of feelings and thoughts because you're grieving the loss of your past life. Try not to judge yourself for any of your feelings.

2. You are not alone. There are millions of men experiencing this challenge right now, and research shows all of them will struggle in some way.

3. You might have thoughts of leaving your situation, but you know that you're strong, and your wife needs you. This guide will give you the tools you need to become a champion carer and husband.

4. Cancer is unique in that people are living with it longer, creating a feeling of indefinite loss. You can be grieving your past life and be uncertain about the future, all while trying to navigate the present.

5. You're on the Hero's Journey right now. This is a quest in which you leave the comfortable past behind, deal with unimaginable trials with the help of others and guides like this one, and make it out the other side a new man.

PART TWO

YOUR MINDSET

Part 2 focuses on your mindset, teaching you how to build courage, control, flexibility, a growth mindset, and gratitude.

Your New Purpose

"A man who becomes conscious of the responsibility he bears toward a human being who affectionately waits for him, or to an unfinished work, will never be able to throw away his life. He knows the 'why' for his existence and will be able to bear almost any 'how.'"
– Viktor Frankl, Man's Search for Meaning

Let's begin Part 2 by articulating your new purpose. The word *purpose* comes from the old French word *por-poser*, which means to put forth or to have an intention. Having a declaration of this intention is powerful because you are stating it to yourself - and the world - that this is the way you'll live from now on. That you have a guiding north star and won't waver from that purpose in the face of difficulty.

You already have a purpose, or multiple purposes, driving you. For some of us that purpose might mean being a great father, or to be a brilliant doctor, or to hike the tallest mountain. You might have more than one purpose that speaks to the core categories of your life: energy, work and love.

Here are two frameworks for understanding how powerful purpose is for us, the first from Viktor Frankl and the second from Simon Sinek.

PURPOSE FRAMEWORK ONE – MAN'S SEARCH FOR MEANING

Viktor Frankl was an Austrian neurologist and psychiatrist who wrote *Man's Search for Meaning.* He wrote this following his time as a prisoner of war in the Second World War, including in the infamous Auschwitz concentration camp.

Frankl, who knew what it meant to suffer, tells us that we can find meaning in any situation, which will give us a reason to push on. His purpose in the camp was to survive so he could be with his wife again, and so he could teach about all he was learning about psychology by being in the camps.

Finding meaning in a cause greater than ourselves is the primary purpose for humans, according to Frankl, and we can find meaning in three sources: doing significant work, love for another and in courage during tough times. We don't need one purpose for our whole life. We can have a purpose guiding us for a single hour or day.

PURPOSE FRAMEWORK TWO – START WITH WHY

Simon Sinek has one of the most widely viewed TED talks globally based on his book, *Start with Why*. Sinek tells us the difference between ordinary and extraordinary companies is that they focus on *why* they exist rather than *what* they do. He uses the example of the Wright Brothers, the first people in the world to achieve powered flight. They were driven by their dream of flying rather than fame or money, while others with the latter focus failed miserably to achieve what the brothers did. Their vision inspired many others to help them, even without payment, and inspired them to push through relentless failure, discomfort and to do it all without a lot of money.

YOUR NEW PURPOSE AND MEANING

You love your wife and she loves you. She needs you now more than ever before. Your purpose is to care for her with all of your capacity and to show her the love Frankl writes about. This sounds easy in theory but is difficult in practice. There is so much out of your control, just like what the concentration camp prisoners faced. They felt the world was against them and didn't care about them or their previous life, no matter who they were before becoming prisoners.

You can no longer gain the same primary sense of purpose from various aspects of your life you used to, such as your work. You don't have the time, energy, or the motivation. This took me a long time to adjust to.

Before Natasha's diagnosis, my top values were to be a great husband and to start my own school. But after a long time struggling to hold on to my past sense of self, I eventually realised my most important purpose was to be the best possible husband, carer and friend for Natasha. Nothing else mattered. Nobody else on earth could do this for her. This was my specific purpose, the mission given to me, should I choose to accept it. The other aspects of my life were still important but were well down the priority list.

As a carer, you must make this shift in your thinking too. Let's explore that now with a short exercise.

EXERCISE: YOUR PURPOSE

Write down your purpose, in terms of how it relates to being a husband and carer, in your own words. What is your unique, specific vocation in this regard? The love and care she receives from you is unique. It is different to that of her siblings, friends or parents.

Are you here because you love your wife and you want to help her to the best of your abilities? Are you here because you'll do everything within your control to make every day as good as it can be for her? What can you add to this? What does this look like in your own words? How does this change your sense of power, control and love?

2.2

Ego is the Enemy

"Almost universally, the kind of performance we give on social media is positive. It is more 'Let me tell you how well things are going. Look how great I am.' It is rarely the truth: 'I am scared. I am struggling. I do not know.'"
- Ryan Holiday, The Ego Is the Enemy

I talk a lot about being a Hero and your first reaction to this term might be that you must become a strong, successful person that everyone admires because of your achievements. Unfortunately, this is the ego talking instead of the heart. In this chapter, we will discuss the ego in more detail: what it is, why it can be a problem, and what to do about it so you can become a true Hero.

What Is The Ego?
Your ego is the part of your mind that creates an image of yourself. It tells the story about who you are: "I'm a hard worker" or "I'm successful" or "I'm...".

Your ego is powerful because we are social animals who are evolved to be around other people, whether for safety or to make life easier. When we were cavemen we had to hunt in groups, and we had to share the load between the village. That meant caring deeply about what others thought of us and whether we had their respect. In a world without money we had to worry about whether we were doing enough for others in return for what they did for us.

This is harder in the modern world. For men, validation can come from how much power we have, how much money we earn, what car we drive, our job title, or how muscular our bodies are.

Why Is The Ego A Problem?

As you take up the role of caring for your wife, you switch your primary purpose to being a husband and carer, as discussed in the previous chapter. You sacrifice focusing on other aspects of your life you previously thought were important, such as your job and your status. But if you cannot work as much or at all anymore, or exercise as much as you used to, the ego starts getting scared, and asks questions like:

"What will people think of me if I'm not working?"

"What will people think of me if I lose my savings?"

"What will people think of me if I…"

There is no external recognition for the hard work you do as a carer. Few people see what you do except your wife, and even she is often too tired to praise you for your efforts. Your ego loves to be rewarded and appreciated, but there is no monetary reward for giving up your life to become a carer. There is no job title that goes on LinkedIn, and the role of carer is unlikely to get you any sort of promotion.

What Can You Do About The Ego?

You must let go of the chains holding you back and build a whole new identity. That new identity is as your wife's carer, and this is your first and foremost identity now. You are becoming the Hero who is a quiet achiever, a silent guardian who isn't out to impress others but who is driven by the desire to become a champion carer and husband. You will become a champion carer and husband, and whether others are impressed or not doesn't matter. You're becoming her Hero and will go to bed each night knowing you did the absolute best job you could do, and the only job you needed to do. The goal is not to impress others, rather it's to impress yourself and to get better each day.

This is a tough lesson for the ego, but that's okay because a job title and recognition are not important. You don't take these with you to the grave. All people will remember of you is how much you loved and were loved. It doesn't matter if your wife forgets to thank you for your efforts, because she needs you to do it all regardless. Your ego is used to having rewards, so train it to act for a deep, inner sense of purpose instead.

One of the best ways to let go of your ego and its voice in your head is through meditation. Meditation, which I cover in more detail in Part 4, is a powerful mental exercise that takes time to get good at. It was by far the most effective way for me to learn to let go. I could shut everything out, listen to that voice in my head questioning my actions, and then quietly and gently tell that voice to go to hell.

You can tell that voice you don't care what people think of you. In fact, most people aren't thinking about you at all anyway. They have enough to deal with in their own lives without worrying about anyone else's. People who judge others for superficial belongings like job titles and the car you drive are not worth knowing anyway. You want to be surrounded by people who love you for the person you are.

That is exactly what you'll be doing for your wife: helping her purely because you love her and not because of any other reason. To do so you'll forget about what your ego thinks is important and instead focus on spending time with your wife and giving her the care she needs, which is all that matters.

2.3

What You Can
and Cannot Control

"James, I cannot control what is happening to my body, but I can control how I respond to it, and nothing has the power to take that control away from me."
– Natasha, 2017

The Stoic philosophy of separating what you can and cannot control is one of the most powerful modes of thinking you can adopt, not just for the situation you're in right now but in all aspects of life.

There is so much outside of your control as a carer that you can quickly become overwhelmed. But if you switch your focus to what you can control, you then feel empowered, strong and influential, even in this toughest of situations.

What Is Outside Your Control?
One reason why cancer is scary is that only the doctors can help

treat it with chemotherapy and radiation but, as a husband, you're unable to do anything at all. You cannot control the pain and discomfort caused by the cancer and the treatment. You cannot even see the cancer, except with scans or fancy equipment, or if it's been surgically removed. This can make you feel completely helpless, which is one of the most painful experiences. I think of the feeling like watching my wife being attacked from a distance, but for some reason being unable to do anything about it. Truly the stuff of nightmares.

Also outside your control is how much time she needs you to spend caring for her, the nurses she has, the emotions of her and others around her, and whether your boss will be sympathetic to the demands of your life as a carer.

What Can You Control?
Thankfully, there is still plenty you can control:

- Your caregiving ability, including learning from this guide;
- Your attitude to changing the way you see your problems;
- Your love for your wife and how you show this to her;
- How you talk to and treat her doctors and nurses;
- How much you learn about the cancer and ask questions;
- How much time and attention you focus on your wife;
- Finding a job where you have a sympathetic boss who gives you flexibility;
- Your reaction to your emotions;
- Your openness with friends and family;
- How much you plan ahead;
- Your thoughts and what you think about and frame the situation;
- Learning from mistakes instead of judging yourself non-stop when they inevitably happen;
- Your own health.

If you think some or any of these aren't within your control right now, over time you'll grow to bring them within your grasp. The good news is that the better you get at focusing on what you can control, the more you find you are in control. Over time you can become a better carer because you are not wallowing in thoughts about how much you cannot control. Instead you are taking charge of everything you can.

A powerful example is taking control over your thoughts. Thoughts are the beginning of everything: thoughts lead to feelings, which lead to actions. The following thoughts will lead you to *not* taking action and thus these become self-fulfilling:

- I *don't* have what it takes to be a great carer;
- I *don't* have control over this situation;
- I *don't* have a normal marriage anymore.

Or, instead, you can choose to focus on thoughts that *empower* you and lead you to *act*:

- I *can* become a great carer;
- I *can* be a great husband;
- I *can* be okay with this situation;
- I *can* be in control of some aspects;
- I *can* be filled with courage despite my fear.

I was initially focused on everything outside my control until I eventually realised I did still have some influence. I began slowly with going to the gym every day, then going out to meet people at job fairs, then learning the Filipino language and culture as I had moved there after the diagnosis. I developed some side projects to earn some money. I started to learn everything I could about Natasha's cancer and how I could help her. I learned more about my emotions and how to help control them. I learned more about how I could adapt to the situation and still do positive activities with Natasha instead of just fixating on having lost our pre-cancer life.

The Serenity Prayer is a prayer Natasha and I would often say together. Even if you don't believe in God, prayer is powerful. Prayer focuses you. You don't have to ask God to grant you serenity and courage. You can ask the universe or yourself. There is still much you can control.

Lord, grant me the courage to change the things which should and can be changed, the serenity to accept the things which cannot be changed, and the wisdom to know the difference.

EXERCISE: CONTROL

What is one thing that is within your control right now, and that you can act on immediately? Could it be something you can say to yourself, like "I've got this"? Something you could say to your wife, like "I'm proud of you and I'm here for you"? Maybe you can simply change a thought you have?

2.4

Flexibility

"Stay committed to your decisions but stay flexible in your approach."
- Tony Robbins

One of the most frustrating aspects of this journey is not living life the way you used to. You've lost your ability to plan ahead and the relationship you once had has changed. For example, I would message Natasha before leaving work to see if I could take her for dinner that night. This would get her out of the house after a day at home and give us some time to do something nice. Many times, however, I would arrive home and find Natasha fast asleep or just not as excited about going out as she had been an hour before when we made plans. The energy required to get ready was often too much.

I had to dig down to what was the ultimate goal of doing so. Was the goal to go out for dinner, or to spend time together, or for

Natasha to spend some time out of the house after a day inside, or to spend time with her away from her parents who we now lived with, or did we want to achieve all of this?

I eventually realised that the true goal had nothing to do with going to a restaurant. My goal was to spend time privately with my wife and to give her a sense of normalcy. So we would go for a drive together. She didn't need to spend energy getting dressed up as nobody would see us in a car, and we could either get drive-through food, or I could order ahead at a restaurant and pick the food up without her having to leave the car. Then we could drive somewhere nice, like to the top of a mountain or to a park, and just sit and chat and eat. We were able to tick every box: having some alone time together, getting Natasha out of the house, and eating a nice dinner! We were both happy with this outcome, even though it was different to our original plan.

Eventually, I learned the importance of flexibility and plenty of creativity. Your goals and solutions will be different to mine but remain flexible. In Part 4 I teach you how meditation will help you notice thoughts before they get a hold of you, and how you can build this flexibility into your work. Quality communication with your wife will help you talk to her about her needs, which is discussed in Part 6.

As always, this won't be easy. There's so much out of your control as a carer that the whole situation can seem hopeless, a feeling that will wear you down. But when you shift the focus to what you can control, and if you're open to being flexible as opposed to holding onto your past life or set plans, you will succeed as a champion husband and carer.

EXERCISE: MAKING NEW PLANS

Think back to a time when a plan you had was changed because of something outside your control. It doesn't have to be related to the cancer.

What are all the reasons you were upset? Not just the surface reason of that plan being cancelled, but what were you trying to achieve with that plan? Recall that my goal of taking Natasha out for dinner was more about spending time with her or taking her out of the house, rather than the dinner itself.

What are some other ways you can achieve those goals? Maybe another plan doesn't tick all of them like your initial plan, but even if it ticks one, that goes a long way for both of you.

2.5

Having A Growth Versus Fixed Mindset

"I've missed more than 9,000 shots in my career. I've lost almost 300 games. 26 times, I've been trusted to take the game-winning shot and missed. I've failed over and over and over again in my life."
- Michael Jordan

"I'm just *not* a carer so I can *never* become great at looking after my wife in the way she needs. I have no idea what I'm doing, and I'll be hopeless at this." Does this sound familiar to you?

You'll probably have some variation of these thoughts. I did, and the thoughts are normal. Treat them as a sign that you love your wife so much you want to be a great carer for her. But if you continually believe you'll never be good at this and the situation is hopeless, then there is a problem. This attitude is a fixed mindset: the belief that your ability to care for your wife is permanently fixed. A fixed mindset is one where you think that because you've never cared for anyone before, and you've never been trained in this, you'll never improve your ability to provide the care your wife needs.

The good news is that it is only your mindset that separates you from believing you can *never* be a great carer and believing you can *become* a great carer. Let's see how this plays out:

- **Scenario 1:** You believe you'll never be a great carer. Therefore you never push yourself to learn and grow and - in turn - will never become a great carer, making your initial belief correct.
- **Scenario 2:** You believe you can become a great carer no matter what, even though this is a new role for you, and you believe you can learn and grow. Therefore, you push yourself to learn and grow, making your new belief also correct.

This second scenario is what is called having a growth mindset. You *believe* you can grow, as simple as that. And because you have this belief, you *do* grow. Here are a few examples of what changes for you when you have a growth mindset:

- You accept you'll make mistakes along the way, because of course you will - you've never done this before!
- You accept you'll initially be disheartened at caring and understanding cancer because you've never had to understand cancer in this way before;
- You accept you'll make mistakes reading and responding to your wife's emotions because you've never experienced these emotions in her before;
- You accept you'll struggle with your own emotions and your

capacity to adapt to the situation because you've never experienced these emotions and this situation before;

- You accept you'll ask pointless questions of the oncologists and surgeons because you've never had to ask these questions before;
- You accept that at times you'll screw up and disappoint yourself and your wife like you've never done before, because this is usually what happens when you're in a new situation.

Your mindset is the only barrier between whether you give up when you make these mistakes, or whether you accept them and keep trying again, forgiving yourself along the way, seeking forgiveness from your wife, talking about your feelings with her and/or with your mates, and surging forth to the next challenge.

After all, this is the Hero's Journey you're on and it's not meant to be easy. What if Frodo gave up when he failed at his first challenge and used this failure as proof he wasn't cut out for this? He would have just returned home and never destroyed the ring. What if Neo in the movie *The Matrix* refused to believe he was the Chosen One because everything was new to him, and just stayed as a coder instead? What if Thomas Edison, America's greatest inventor gave up after his thousands of mistakes? He would never have invented the light bulb. In fact, Edison called these setbacks *learning experiences* rather than *mistakes*. Natasha would correct me whenever I admonished myself, telling me that I never made mistakes, I just had a whole heap of learning experiences.

Many people are afraid of new challenges because they're afraid of making mistakes. Mistakes are scary because humans worry about being judged by those around us. The fear mechanism in your mind, which occurs in the amygdala, is still there after all these thousands of years of evolution. The best you can do is recognise the fear and then just go ahead anyway.

Go ahead and make the mistake because mistakes are a natural part of learning. If you don't make a mistake when learning, then you already knew how to do the task and aren't learning anything new. When you stretch yourself from what you know - and what you are capable of right now - to where you want to be in the future, you are journeying on an unknown path.

Unfortunately, the mainstream education system most people have grown up in often drills in a fear of mistakes. When a child raises their hand to answer a question and gets it wrong, some teachers will make them feel bad for not paying attention or for not thinking their answer through properly. Plus, when there are 30 other students in a classroom, making a mistake is embarrassing, so most people will just keep quiet and wait for the student who already knows the answer. School struggles to inspire people to follow their natural curiosity.

Imagine if school tried to teach people how to ride a bike. First, we would go to class, open the textbook, have a teacher talk at us, then give us an exam. Then, maybe, we'd actually get the chance to get on the bike!

This is nothing like how people learn to ride a bike in the real world. To learn how to ride, we'd just jump on the bike because we had a strong desire to learn. And every single one of us fell off. Then we might have put training wheels on the bike to ease into it. Then the training wheels came off and we would fall off again. And again. And again. But everyone who ever went through this process can now ride a bike and can do so without thinking consciously about it and without fear.

This is exactly what you'll go through when learning to care for your wife. It's tempting to berate yourself when you make a mistake. Maybe you didn't ask the right questions of the doctor. Maybe you forgot to turn up to an appointment. Maybe you picked an unsuitable doctor. Perhaps you didn't help your wife up in the right way and caused her more pain. Maybe you were tired and couldn't hear her asking for help. Maybe you didn't know the right words to say when she was feeling upset. Maybe you were overwhelmed by everything and couldn't make a critical decision.

These are just some of the mistakes you might make on your learning journey. But you don't have to let them define you. You can be grateful for making the mistake because you won't do it again. Learn from it.

Acknowledge And Apologise For Your Mistakes
Apologise to your wife if you make a mistake and tell her you've learned from it. Tell her in person rather than over text. Focus on the apology rather than an explanation although you can give a brief one if you like. Spend time listening to her response. You'll often find she is just filled with gratitude for you being there and caring for her in the best way you can.

Be Grateful For Your Mistakes
Instead of beating yourself up next time you stuff up, tell yourself that you're learning how to become a champion caregiver. That you're grateful for the opportunity to learn from this and to level up. That who you are or what you did in the past is not who you are now or in the future. That you are your wife's carer and this is the hardest job you'll ever have to do for her. That you've never done this before, so be easy on yourself.

Be Okay With Sounding Stupid

I like to ask questions even if they make me sound stupid because I don't care if I sound stupid. If I don't know something, what's the point of feeling embarrassed? There's no way I can ever know everything in this world so why pretend I do? I studied very different disciplines than medicine, so why would I be expected to know anything about this discipline?

I like to approach life like a child. They ask questions about everything, all the time, because they're genuinely curious and must learn as much as they can to survive in this world. Likewise, you must put your pride behind you to become a champion carer. Once you're over your irrational fear of sounding stupid, you can ask any question you like.

You'll always make mistakes, even when you're a champion carer, because your wife's situation will always be changing, and you must therefore always adapt and learn. A champion carer can never do everything perfectly; nobody is perfect. Instead they pick themselves up, analyse what happened, and put steps in place to try not to let the mistake happen again. Because you're reading this book, you already have a growth mindset and are willing to learn.

2.6

Perfectionism

"The all-or-nothing mind-set leads perfectionists to transform every setback they encounter into a catastrophe, an assault on their very worth as human beings. Their sense of self inevitably suffers as their fault-finding turns inward."
- Tal Ben-Shahar, Being Happy

You probably have a goal to become the perfect cancer carer for your wife. This sounds great but the goal is problematic because it's impossible to be perfect. I used to be a perfectionist, and was proud of this, until a psychologist helped me realise how perfectionism was holding me back in life.

No one will ever be perfect. What does 'perfect' even mean? If it's about being the perfect money-maker then you'll never achieve perfection because there will always be someone else with more money. If you were the richest guy on earth, there would still be something else you were missing. Maybe perfection means to have perfect looks, but what does that even mean? Everyone admires different aspects of a person and looks fade. What about perfect health? That means you would live forever. So is not a possible outcome either.

What about being the perfect husband? That would mean never making a mistake and at every second knowing exactly what your wife needed from you. You'd be earning a high salary, never think about any other women, satisfy your wife in every single way she could imagine, be an excellent cook, never get angry with the children and - while earning that high salary - spend as much time with your family as you wished. Does this even seem possible? It's thoroughly impossible and you shouldn't even bother attempting to be the perfect husband or you'll be constantly disappointed.

But what if the goal was not to be the perfect husband, but a great husband? Suddenly you can be human again because you recognise failure as a possibility. You'll make mistakes. Suddenly you're allowed to be too tired to have sex, can lose your temper at a child when you don't mean to, or you can work late a few nights to put food on the table for your family. When you aim for greatness instead of perfection, you're doing your best but are limited by your humanity. Being human means you have emotions. You get tired. You get angry. You cannot be in three places at once. You only have two hands. You make mistakes. You're not your wife's or children's mind-reader. You say things you regret. You say things you didn't know would hurt the other person.

And that this is okay. Your wife will love you because you're trying your best. And God doesn't want you to be perfect (if you believe in God) because God loves you anyway. The goal was never perfection.

What would it mean to be the perfect cancer carer instead of the best carer you can be? You would have all the following attributes of a perfect carer (while also being the perfect husband). Instead, aim to be the best possible carer:

The Perfect versus The Best Possible Carer	
The Perfect Carer	**The Best Possible Carer**
The knowledge and experience of an oncologist	You learn as much as you can about your wife's cancer with the limited time you have
The knowledge and experience of a medical nurse	You learn how to treat your wife for small issues and take her to hospital for big ones
The caring experience of a hospice nurse	You learn how to lift and wash and dress your wife when she needs you to
The stoicism of a monk	You learn to separate what you can and cannot control
The ability to juggle multiple roles all at once	You do your best with each role you have, one at a time

If you're aiming to be the perfect carer or the perfect husband, put this book down now and stop reading because it's impossible. It's far more realistic to aim to be the best possible carer. Be open to learning and making mistakes along the way. You'll never even try to be a great carer and husband if you only do so with a guarantee of perfect success. One of the great dangers of perfectionism is that it holds people back from taking a chance and doing something new. Your protective mind knows perfectionism is impossible so it tricks you into only ever attempting something scary if guaranteed to do it perfectly. Knowing how impossible this is, you choose not to do the new task and shrink back into safety, right where your mind wants you to be.

Letting go of perfectionism actually frees you. You're free to explore and try new ways of operating. You're free to not fear failing or criticism or the judgment of others. You're free to put your own mark on this journey.

2.7

Courage As An
Antidote To Fear

*"Choose not to be harmed—and you will not feel harmed.
Do not feel harmed—and you have not been."*
- Marcus Aurelius

The champion carer's journey will bring about strong feelings of fear. The hardest part to understand is you cannot make the fear go away. Fear is one of those aspects outside of your conscious control, even though it's a feeling inside you. Every day you'll experience some kind of fear, including fear of:

- What the latest scans will show;
- How your wife will cope with the latest round of chemo;
- How you'll keep everything together;
- The next meeting with doctors;
- The intense feelings of grief you're already experiencing;
- The lack of control you feel.

All of this is normal and understandable, even if no one else can grasp how you're feeling. Knowing that a range of fears is normal doesn't help you practically as you venture forward though. Your wife needs you to care for her, no matter how afraid you are.

One reaction to acknowledging these fears exist could be to eliminate them and get on with the job of caring. This is not an option. Fear is impossible to eliminate because it's one of the strongest emotions you can feel. You have enough active battles without trying to combat something as powerful and deep-rooted as your fear.

Here is what must be done instead: everything. Acknowledge your fears and do what needs doing regardless while carrying those fears along with you. How do you do this? With courage. Heroic courage. Probably the most courage you've ever needed. An analogy can be drawn with soldiers going to war. Soldiers of course feel fear but their job requires them to do go to war anyway. They cannot fight the enemy without engaging them. The enemy won't wait for their fear to go away either. They cannot say, "Hold on mate, let me sort myself out; don't kill me for a second, and when I'm ready then we can fight!" That's not the way a war, or the world, works. The clock is ticking. Instead of getting rid of the fear, soldiers fight anyway, with heroic courage, not knowing what will happen.

Fear is an emotion that tells you you're faced with the need to step up to a new level, one outside your safe comfort zone. If you only ever did what was safe, you would never be where you are now. Humanity would never have new inventions because inventors would be too afraid of the risk. Humanity would be safe but not pushing the boundaries in any way at all. Fear is what kept humans safe for thousands of years in the wild and protected them from being eaten by animals. Fear keeps you alive in new or unfamiliar situations, but you're not living in the wild anymore. There came a point for those ancient humans when, despite the fear, they needed to feed their families, so they had to go out and hunt. They had to carry the fear with them and go out anyway.

The way I overcome fear is by treating the voice in my head like it's coming from a separate part of my mind that hasn't evolved to realise I'm not living in the wild anymore. Let's call it Lizard Mind. I thank the Lizard Mind for doing its job and then tell it I've got this. Then it starts to learn that yes, indeed, you do have this under control. Lizard Mind starts to learn that you're much more capable than it was giving you credit for. You appreciate it looking out for you but you have a wife to care for. You cannot hide away. You're forging ahead and Lizard Mind can come with you, like it or not. It cannot believe how much courage you're able to muster in the worst situation possible. It starts to redefine your comfort zone and expand your toolkit for dealing with the situation. You'll make plenty of mistakes and Lizard Mind will keep coming back to tell you "I told you so", but you can learn to put it aside. In time, Lizard Mind will shut up and watch you push on anyway, helpless to stop you with your newfound courage and caregiving talent. In fact, Lizard Mind is actually silently applauding you for doing what it thought was impossible.

Heroes are not those who eliminate their fear. They are those who acknowledge their fear and develop the courage to push on regardless. You are that heroic husband and carer who is stepping up in the face of immense fear and uncertainty.

2.8

Mindfulness
And The Present

"We can only connect the dots looking back."
– Steve Jobs

Grappling with the loss of the future and the past life you had is a major challenge during this journey, as explored earlier in the discussion on indefinite loss in Chapter 1.2. One way to help you cope with this is by focusing on the present.

Life is a series of moments connected together. They probably don't make sense right now, but you can only ever connect the dots looking back, as Steve Jobs, co-founder of Apple, told us in his Stanford University graduation speech.

Natasha and I spent two years in the Philippines after she was diagnosed, which made no sense at all at the time. I had to adapt to a foreign culture, learn a new language and I didn't know anyone there except Natasha's family. I didn't have a job. Over the two years, though, I did find work and new friends, so much so that I was reluctant to return to Australia for fear of starting all over again.

My time in Manila made sense looking back though, when I saw how I was formed into a businessman and entrepreneur, pushed out of my comfort zone and into a new career path. Out of the friends I made in Manila, one of them is now my co-founder of The School Transformation Group, an education consultancy we started. None of this could have happened but for our time in the Philippines, and the dots lined up in a way I could never have predicted.

I have no idea about my own future now. None of us do. All I'm focused on right now is writing these words to help other men like you who are in the situation I was in. Writing this book feels right in this moment, and I have no idea where this will lead. That lack of knowing used to scare me, but it's surprisingly reassuring. All I can control is what I do right now and my reactions right now.

A mindset of embracing uncertainty is vital for your relationship with your wife. You have no idea what will happen in the future as it's mostly out of your control, just as the past cannot be changed no matter what you do. All that's important is the time you have with your wife right now. If you get caught up worrying about an uncertain future, you are taking up valuable thinking and feeling capacity that you could be directing to your life right now.

Your life in the present moment probably doesn't make any sense, and I know this feeling only too well. You must have faith and hope that everything will eventually make sense. I'm yet to understand why Natasha died though; that dot is still unclear.

What I do know is I had a fantastic marriage with her and grew as a man in a way I could not have done without her. She was the best example of someone living in the moment, grateful for every day and happy with small pleasures. She gave up worrying about the future so it wouldn't destroy her happiness in the moment. Natasha was so successful at being happy that everyone who met her knows she did indeed live a full life. She lived a life others only dream of, and there are plenty of people who live three times as long as she did who are utterly miserable, usually because they are caught up in regret for the past or fear for the future.

Live in a way that, regardless if today was the last day you were alive, you would definitely be happy. The only way to do that is to be fully present in the moment, right now.

This is the essence of mindfulness: bringing joy into the present. You can start right now by bringing your attention to the present and letting go of the past and future. To help you get better at this, you can learn more about meditation in chapter 4.1. Living in the present is a choice. It's a difficult one but this approach to life will make a major difference to the way you live.

2.9

The Practice
Of Gratitude

*"When you are grateful, fear disappears,
and abundance appears."*
– Tony Robbins

What could you possibly be grateful for when everything seems so hard? The short answer is that there's plenty to be grateful for. Focusing on this will shift your whole experience of the cancer journey. Focusing on gratitude helps to reduce your fear and helps you to become happier. Being grateful doesn't automatically make your wife better, but it does change your mindset.

After I started practising gratitude, my whole worldview changed. I realised this process can be used for anything: our job, our possessions, and our body. With your body, you might think you can only be happy once you have five percent body fat, six-pack abs and bulging biceps. But why not be grateful to have a healthy body? This mindset shift helps us to be happy right now, rather than waiting to be happy. With your job, you might think you can only be happy when you have your boss' job or become a famous CEO, but can you choose to be grateful right now for the job you do have and the income it provides right now?

My first thought when I learned about gratitude is that if I focus on gratitude for what I already have, then wouldn't this reduce my ambition to strive for more? If I'm already grateful for having reasonable health, then what's the point of working out? If I'm grateful for the job I already have, won't I lose my ambition to work harder?

These are typical reactions, but does being grateful for what you already have or who you are stop you from striving for being better? Not at all. In fact, gratitude actually helps us achieve those ambitions because we are more joyful and loving of ourselves in the process.

For example, someone might work out every morning because they have the goals of one day achieving great muscle tone, a low resting heart rate and enhanced flexibility. These are worthy goals to aim for but if they told themselves they would only be happy when that happens, then it's harder to be happy right now. Instead, every time they come home from the gym, they could switch their mindset to be grateful that they actually have the health and energy to move and work out, or for the instant boost to their happiness from the exercise. This gratitude can make them happy right now, without holding back from their ambitious goals. They can be happy when they achieve their goal as well as being happy right now. It's like the saying of having your cake and eating it too, although I have always been confused as to why you would have cake without eating it!

This takes us to the cancer carer journey: you might think there is nothing you can be grateful for; and that you'll only be happy when your wife gets better and your life can go back to normal. That will no doubt make you happy, and you shouldn't stop hoping and working hard for this outcome. But how can you be happy right now, despite how hard everything is?

EXERCISE: GRATITUDE

What are you grateful for right now? And what are you grateful for in yourself? Some ideas:

- Your marriage;
- Your commitment and discipline to being a great carer and husband;
- The love you have for each other and all your great memories;
- Having a house to live in;
- Your energy and strength to care for your wife;
- The care your wife's doctors and nurses are giving her;
- Medical research as well as hospitals with their fancy machines and medicines that can achieve results which were impossible even twenty years ago.

You could do this exercise with your wife and come up with a list together. Perhaps even start by telling her you are grateful for having her in your life, because often she will feel like she is holding you back.

You could do this exercise with your wife and come up with a list together. Perhaps even start by telling her you are grateful for having her in your life, because often she will feel like she is holding you back.

Think about this gratitude list and add to it, every day. Take a minute before going to sleep to go over the list alone in your head, or chat about it with your wife. I like going over my list in the morning because it helps me start the day happy. You could do both - it's entirely up to you.

Rather than focusing only on how awful everything is, shift your focus to include the blessings you have. Some days you'll have to push hard to think of these blessings, but there is always at least one part of your day you can be grateful for.

You always have a choice. You can choose to be ungrateful and only focus on the negatives which will make you stay miserable. Or you can choose to be happier right now, even when there seems to be nothing going right at all. If you cannot control what is happening around you, you may as well make a choice that helps aim you towards joy rather than only feeling sorrow.

KEY POINTS FROM PART 2

- Know you can come back to a deep sense of purpose and meaning in this role when it gets tough. You get to define and orient your purpose towards being a champion carer and husband.

- Your ego will try to hold you back in making this shift. It will ask you what other people will think of you when you shift your priorities away from what everyone else is focused on. You have the power to deliberately ignore that voice and to tell a different story.

- There is much outside of your control, so you will feel helpless much of the time, but focusing on the feeling will only lead to frustration. Instead, focus on what you can control - and there is still plenty.

- Flexibility helps in making these adjustments and recognising you cannot hold onto your past routines.

- Adopt a growth mindset, which is where you recognise that even if you've never been a carer, you can learn anything you put your mind to.

- Always aim for being the good-enough carer, because perfection is impossible.

- You'll feel a tremendous amount of fear in this journey and you cannot make fear disappear. Instead you can control your response to the fear, which is not to let the fear cripple you and to do the job anyway.

- To deal with fear about the future and grief about the past, orient yourself towards the present. Practise focusing on the present to help with this.

- There is still at least one part of your day you can be grateful for. Focus on this instead of how bad everything is.

PART THREE

YOU ARE
NEVER ALONE

This part of the book is about how to care for yourself by finding help from others. It covers who could help you, how to find them, and how to ask for help.

You Are Never Alone

"The most terrible poverty is loneliness."
– Mother Teresa

Getting help from others will be one of the most important things you can do for yourself and your wife. It's tempting to think you can go on this journey alone, but this isn't realistic. Part 3 explores the problems faced in admitting you need help and how you can get that help.

The Problem: Men Find It Difficult To Reach Out For Help
It's all too common for men to feel isolated when they become husband carers, which is one reason this book is aimed only at men. Research shows that women typically find it easier to reach out for help. Like most men, you want to believe you have everything together and don't need others to help protect and defend yourself and your wife. You don't want to appear weak to

others. You want to appear strong for your wife and not add to her burden.

In the social media world, it's tempting to put up the façade that everything is great in your world and to make others envious of you. This makes it even harder to reach out and admit that, actually, everything is not fine.

Often I felt I couldn't rely on Natasha to provide much support for me, no matter how much she wanted to. She had limited energy and had to save that to focus on herself. Sometimes I wanted to confide in Natasha how I was feeling, but I then looked at her lying in bed exhausted after a week of chemotherapy, and felt isolated. I felt like I was sitting there helpless, with nobody to talk to, not even my wife.

Nobody knows what you're experiencing unless they've been through this situation themselves. Even then, every situation is unique. You'll find that few people, even doctors, will know what to say or do to help you. Some doctors I have spoken to are not aware of the difficulties facing partners, and the limited time they have with patients means they cannot check in with you. Initially, when everything was such a blur of chaos, I felt that my friends didn't care about me because they weren't communicating much. This made me feel worse and more isolated.

The Truth: You Must Reach Out For Help No Matter How Hard This Is

Reaching out to people will help you more than you can imagine. The number one breakthrough for me was eventually realising I could open up to my family and friends and realising they would do anything to help me. It might be a simple hello from you, but your support team is out there ready to get in touch when you're ready. Knowing you're never alone, even if nobody you know is experiencing what you are, is one of the most powerful and comforting messages you can hear right now.

After Natasha passed away, a good friend told me they had no idea what I needed from them even though they wanted to help and do anything to support me. All I had to do was communicate this to them. But I found this hard. Often even I had no idea what I needed. Most of the time I just needed companionship such as having a meal with friends or going on a bushwalk together. Whatever it was, as soon as I told my friends and family what I needed, they went over and above to do that for me.

When you have so much happening in your life, how on earth can you be expected to communicate with others? How can you make this easy on yourself? Let's look at some strategies to help you connect with those who can help you.

Using A Group Email Strategy
In the early days of Natasha's illness, all I wanted was a few messages of support or a phone call. I didn't have time for more than this because everything was intense and chaotic with surgery, chemotherapy and the move to a new country. The easiest method I found was to send a group email to my closest friends and family.

I recommend an email instead of social media. With email, you can go into depth about everything and you don't then need to repeat yourself to every single person you talk to. On social media you're connected with many people who are not your closest friends or are only acquaintances, and they won't be as helpful. They might say something nice in a comment, or 'like' a post, but you need proper and meaningful support at this point in your life. I recommend emailing your closest supporters, which is what I called my close friends and family who I knew truly cared. You can open up to your supporters, rather than posting on social media where people usually hide the truth. This still takes a huge amount of vulnerability, but is always worth it.

Before the cancer I had never been open with people apart from Natasha. Eventually, I found that the more I opened up about my feelings and fears, the closer my relationships became, and the better my supporters were able to help out.

A surprising effect of sharing my struggles was that many of my friends opened up to me about their struggles too. One good friend was moving to a new city on the other side of Australia and was anxious about not finding work. He felt bad for telling me because he didn't think his situation was as awful as mine. I told him there was not much worse than what I was experiencing, but if he was feeling terribly anxious then we were in the same boat. We ended up helping each other get through our own struggles with the techniques we were each using. Other friends would open up about struggles they had with their jobs, families or in general about their life.

Why should you open up with friends and deal with all their struggles on top of your own? It's not to solve these problems, because you cannot, and they cannot solve yours. The point instead is to share with someone the pains and struggles of life and realise everyone has something they're dealing with. None of us are living perfect lives, but when you're caught up in the sometimes-unbearable pain of seeing your wife sick and caring for her, you can feel easily like you're the only one who is struggling.

You're never alone, so reach out and open up. Ease into this. Share that you're feeling angry about your wife's diagnosis. Of course you're angry, and so are your supporters, so your sharing this won't be wildly out of the blue. If anything, they would probably be surprised if you weren't angry! Admitting your feelings and starting to share them will do more for your coping capacity, and therefore your caring capacity, than you can imagine.

The Better You Cope, The Better Your Wife Copes

If you're looked after and feeling okay, then you'll be better able to support your wife in the unique way she needs. I would give my supporters an insight into what was happening, whether it was surgery or chemo or having a break and doing something nice. Then I would tell them how I was feeling. I would sometimes tell them how Natasha was feeling and coping, but often I would leave this up to her to tell her own supporters. In a way, I made this communication mainly about my journey because what I needed from my supporters would be different to what Natasha needed. Most of the time she didn't have the energy to take phone calls or write emails anyway, and the only support she needed was mine.

A word of caution before you proceed: ask for permission from your wife about what you want to share. There may be information she doesn't want anyone to know about, despite you thinking it isn't that big of a deal. For example, I would tell Natasha that, 'I'm thinking of telling my friends you're okay at the moment but the last chemo session was super tough, is that okay?' and most of the time she would say yes. A couple of times I shared some information and forgot to ask her whether it was okay, and she got upset as she felt I had shared something too personal. What I thought was okay to share was sometimes different to how she was thinking. Your wife's emotions and energy levels will be all over the place, and something she thinks is okay one week might not be the next - all part of how tough this journey is for you!

You don't need permission, however, to be personal about how *you're* feeling.

EXERCISE: YOUR FIRST EMAIL TO SUPPORTERS
- This might be your first time sharing feelings or a group email like this, so let's do a practice run in a safe space here.
- Write down a list of the people you consider to be your supporters: people you know you can count on no matter what. Your closest family and friends, or perhaps even a friend you've lost touch with over the years, which was the case for me. This can be an opportunity to reconnect with them.
- Jot down a couple of things you want to share with them, for example:
  - What is happening with the cancer treatment at the moment?
  - What is your routine like these days?
  - Are you still working?
- Draft the email. You don't have to send it just yet.
- Chat about the email with your wife and let her know what you are saying.
- Send it when you're ready.

Other Methods To Get Help

It's okay if you aren't ready to share with your supporters. Sometimes you don't want to share your fears and emotions with those closest to you. Sometimes you want to keep intimate details of your marriage close to your heart. Sometimes, no matter how supportive your family and friends are, they have no idea what to say. This is when professional support can help. There are plenty of other people and organisations you can reach out to. Even if you think you're fine, and you may well be fine, it's still worth reaching out. The other benefit of this is when you do hit an emotional crisis during your journey, you know you've made the call in the past so it's nothing new to you.

Try calling a helpline which helps with mental health support, suicide prevention services and emotional assistance. You can search for 'lifeline' in your country, and there is a Wikipedia page entitled 'List of suicide crisis lines', which gives you options for your country. You might not be thinking suicidal thoughts, so ignore the title of that Wikipedia page, but the helplines are designed for anyone in a crisis. I hesitated before first calling them because I felt everything was okay, but as soon as I started to tell the phone counsellor what I was feeling, I felt a wave of release and relief. This was all held up inside without me knowing.

Your country or hospital might have in-person, online or phone support groups for carers. I used a phone service a few times, which was convenient as I didn't have to leave Natasha alone to go to a support group. I could chat anonymously with the others. Hearing other people's stories directly was reassuring. Being told by a doctor or psychologist that every carer goes through the same emotions and troubles is not the same as talking with other carers.

You Are Never Alone
Your wife has been diagnosed with one of the worst diseases known to humans and your life has been turned upside down. It would be ridiculous and delusional to pretend everything is okay! Your friends might be more worried if you did pretend. Instead, they would consider it a sign of strength to admit you need a bit of a chat, even if it's about something that feels normal, like your favourite sport or the latest headlines. To pretend everything is

okay and not confront the reality will make this journey far harder than it needs to be.

3.2

Seeking Professional Help

"What is distinctive about therapy is what it is a tool for: it is an invention to help improve the way our emotions operate."
– The School of Life

The idea of seeing a medical professional about mental health issues can be daunting. There can be fears about opening up to someone about your life. Seeing a therapist might lead to some or all of the following thoughts:

- Why would talking about my issues help me?
- Surely psychologists are for crazy people?
- What will my friends think if they find out I'm seeing a shrink?
- I can only get help from a real doctor, not a psychologist;
- I have no idea how psychologists work, so I will stick to what I know;
- I can solve the problem myself without help.

It's common for carers to put off finding help because life doesn't seem that bad at the moment. I'd never seen a doctor about mental health before Natasha was diagnosed, so it was all new to me. I had many of the same thoughts above about the process and delayed finding help until I hit rock bottom. Research shows this to be common for cancer carers.

What changed my thoughts about getting professional help was seeing a doctor who told me to call Lifeline in Australia. This advice came a whole year after the diagnosis and he was the first doctor Natasha and I saw who checked in and asked how I was feeling rather than focusing solely on Natasha as the cancer patient. We weren't even seeing him about the cancer - he was assessing Natasha for something else. He asked me to get a blood test to test my own general health and then to come back to him alone, without Natasha.

I didn't think anything of his request until I returned to follow up on the results. He asked how I was doing and explained that I had to prioritise my mental health in this situation. I couldn't stop myself crying in front of him, no matter how hard I tried, and then he gave me Lifeline's number to call so that I knew they were there. I did that and couldn't stop crying either. All the emotions of the past year, that I had bottled up, were uncontrollably released. I couldn't remember the last time I had cried. It had been that long.

The idea of possibly crying in front of someone might put you off seeing a doctor, but hopefully you are instead encouraged to do so. You probably don't have any other avenue to do this because you want to hide tears and your struggle from your wife and family or you don't have time alone anymore. You might not cry when seeing the doctor, but at least you'll have the chance to talk to a medical professional.

See A Doctor

I recommend seeing the same GP or family doctor as your wife so that you don't have to re-explain your situation to them. They keep everything confidential as though you're separate patients. You don't need to worry about what you say. If you don't feel comfortable opening up with your wife's GP, though, then find another one.

When booking to see a new GP, look on the practice website for their doctors' specialties or ask the receptionist to see a doctor who specialises in men's mental health. When I moved to Melbourne after Natasha passed away, I did this and luckily found a brilliant and supportive GP who worked tirelessly to help me through the grieving process. Unfortunately, I found my previous regular GPs, including Natasha's GP, not as easy for me to open up to.

Go to a practice where you can see the same GP regularly, rather than those where you queue up and see the first available one. You need someone constant by your side.

AS SOON AS POSSIBLE, IF NOT RIGHT NOW, BOOK AN APPOINTMENT TO SEE A GP

Tell them what you're experiencing and, if they are competent, they will give you a mental health questionnaire to complete which is similar to the one at the end of this chapter. If you're in Australia, they will put you on a mental health-care plan that entitles you to rebates for seeing a psychologist. They will then, if more experienced in mental health care, recommend a psychologist for you to see or at least a practice that has good psychologists. Some GPs, like my Melbourne one, will recognise if something is seriously wrong and prescribe antidepressant and/or anti-anxiety medication.

Antidepressants And Other Medication

Prescribed medication works when a need is identified, but many people are resistant to it. An analogy to help overcome this resistance is your wife taking chemotherapy medication to fight the cancer. The research is constantly evolving in the field of antidepressants and is already advanced. The drugs work in different ways, depending on what you need help with. Some medications I took were designed to help me sleep better, others were prescribed to keep me awake. The strongest one I took had to be prescribed by a psychiatrist and essentially stopped my thoughts at night just so I could sleep.

If your doctor prescribes medication, ask them any questions you have, for example about side-effects, how the medication works and why they recommend it. Don't see it as a sign of weakness if you need this help. Help can come in many forms, and this is a powerful one.

Only doctors can prescribe this medication, such as your GP or a psychiatrist. Some psychologists can prescribe, but if they cannot they'll recommend you go back to your GP and ask them to prescribe medication for you. One psychologist I saw wrote a letter to my GP explaining why she found it vital for me to go on medication.

Finally, you don't have to be afraid of becoming addicted to the medication. Your GP and psychologist will work with you to wean you off the medication when you are ready. Think of the medication as an emergency stopgap to get you well enough to function until you are ready to keep going without the help.

Seeing A Therapist (Psychologist Or Social Worker)
This can be far more daunting than seeing a GP because most of us have seen a GP before, but few have ever seen a therapist. Think of the need to see a specialist like your wife's need to see an oncologist. She had never needed one before this situation but she now needs that particular type of specialist. A therapist is a specialist for mental health, which is a real disease. They have years of rigorous training and only deploy scientifically-proven methods of helping you cope.

Hopefully your GP will recommend a therapist they know is suitable and good. If not, it can be difficult to know how to find a good one. Even with online ratings, a therapist who works well for one person might not work well for you. The most straightforward method to find one is to look for a reputable practice with multiple psychologists under one roof. This works well because the practice will have done its own vetting for quality therapists, and the receptionists can point you to the most suitable therapist based on a few questions they ask. They might ask if you prefer a male or female and, although I have only ever seen female therapists, trust your gut instinct.

Your first session will mostly be them getting to know you and will be about an hour or an hour and a half. You probably won't walk away feeling better after one session, so don't expect a quick fix. Much will come up in your sessions with a therapist and this takes time. Be patient and be prepared to open up as nothing you say to them will ever leave the room unless in the extremely rare case that a court requires it.

Some cancer hospitals have social workers available. They don't have the rigorous training psychologists have but are usually more affordable or free if part of the hospital's holistic care. They also have experience with the unique issues related to cancer, so you might find them even better than a general psychologist. Keep experimenting to see what works for you.

If The Doctor Or Psychologist Is Not Working Out, Find A New One

Make a switch if you are not getting along well with the doctor or psychologist you're seeing. Not every personality will click with you, so be open to trying a new doctor or psychologist until you find the right one for you. I judge them by how much they genuinely care, rather than going through routine motions, and by how comfortable I feel opening up with them about my issues. Thankfully I have mostly had brilliant therapists, but there were a few who I realised weren't specialised in what I was experiencing or who I couldn't easily open up to.

A major part of the Hero's Journey is having help along the way. If there are people out there whose speciality is helping people in a crisis, it would be more foolish not to see those specialists than to pretend you have everything together.

You cannot wait for life to go drastically wrong before seeking help. That's what I did and it's not worth it. Your wife needs you to be in the best condition - physically and emotionally - that you can be. Thankfully, you can get help for both. You might think you have everything under control but often this is the mind's protective mechanism kicking in. There aren't many crises in life a man will have to go through which are worse than the situation you're in, so don't put off getting help just because you might think you're okay.

EXERCISE: A SELF-ASSESSMENT.

Tick the boxes or write your answer down for each question in your notebook. This is purely for your reflection.

In the last 2 weeks...	Never	Occasionally	Sometimes	Most of the time	Always
About how often did you feel tired out for no good reason?					
About how often did you feel nervous?					
About how often did you feel so nervous that nothing could calm you down?					
About how often did you feel hopeless?					
About how often did you feel restless or fidgety?					

In the last 2 weeks...	Never	Occasionally	Sometimes	Most of the time	Always
About how often did you feel so restless you could not sit still?					
About how often did you feel depressed?					
About how often did you feel everything was an effort?					
About how often did you feel so sad nothing could cheer you up?					
About how often did you feel worthless?					
About how often did you feel out of control with your anger?					

KEY POINTS FROM PART 3

1. Book in to see a doctor (GP or family doctor) as soon as possible.

2. You are never alone, even if you might feel that way.

3. Recognise that seeking help from your supporters and medical professionals is the strong and courageous choice.

4. People want to help you, but often don't know how, so open up and tell them what you need.

5. Try to limit your communication to your closest family and friends who will be your supporters through this.

6. The easiest method of communicating with them is with a group email in order to avoid repeating yourself to everyone.

7. Experiment with seeing a therapist.

PART FOUR

CARING FOR YOU

In Part 4 we discuss the practical tools to help you care for yourself, such as diet, sleep and powerful habits.

Two Powerful Habits

"In forty-five years of work as a consultant I have not come across a single natural, an executive who was born effective. All the effective ones have had to learn to be effective. And all of them had to practise effectiveness until it became a habit."
– Peter Drucker, The Effective Executive

In this chapter I discuss two of the most powerful habits you can add to your life. They will seem like chores and a burden at first, because they are, so I'll show you a process for installing them. If the habits were easy to follow then everyone would be doing them, but they aren't easy. You're becoming a champion carer, so this is one of many difficult steps along the journey.

Your goal is to have as many of these habits running on autopilot as possible so you don't have to think about them and can instead focus on caring for your wife.

What Is A Habit?

A habit is something you do unconsciously or with little effort. They can be good or bad. Think of brushing your teeth. You do this out of habit as part of your morning and evening routine so you don't have to muster up the will to brush your teeth every day. Not brushing your teeth would feel weird. Yet when you first learned how to brush your teeth you needed constant reminders. We also all have bad habits; habits you didn't always have but are hard to get rid of because of how ingrained they become. Compulsively checking a smartphone or unconsciously opening a beer every night are examples of bad habits.

How Do Habits Work?

Good habits are hard to build and can take a long time to install yet are easy to lose. Habits can either be time-based or triggered by something beforehand regardless of the time performed. Going for a jog every day is an example of a time-based habit. A trigger habit is something done as soon as something else is done, for example putting on a seatbelt when getting into the car. You never think about this and you put on the seatbelt even if you only seldom drive a car.

Your wife's situation is unpredictable so you want to make as much of your life run on autopilot as possible, just like your body automating breathing and digestion to free up brainpower for other functions. What comes next are two of the most powerful habits to help you become a champion carer and husband: meditation and journaling.

HABIT 1 – MEDITATION

Why Meditate

Meditation might seem like something only monks in isolated monasteries do as a purely spiritual exercise, but it was by far the most beneficial activity for me coping. The idea of being a strong man might not fit with something that seems so touchy-feely. You might think it's a sign of strength to disregard emotions and that meditating is a sign of weakness. I had these thoughts about meditation too but the more I tried it, the more I realised it was actually giving me more strength. Then when I started reading about how Navy SEALs - the toughest soldiers there are - meditate to help them in combat, I realised this practice is not just for sissies.

The primary reason to meditate is because, at times, you'll feel overwhelmed by your thoughts and emotions. At any one time, you could be feeling scared, lonely, sad, angry, exhausted and confused. These feelings could then come out in different ways. You build up a short temper, isolate yourself, make simple mistakes, or lose the ability to make good decisions.

On top of these feelings, you'll have many other thoughts too. You could be thinking about plans for your wife when she needs to go to hospital, how to balance work and caring, how to tell friends and family about what's happening, how you can show your wife more love, or when to find time to buy her medicines, groceries or unwind with your mates. Imagine you have all these feelings and thoughts all at once; you can easily see how you could quickly become overwhelmed. This overload of feelings and thoughts can then lead to the point of developing a severe mental illness like depression or anxiety.

What Meditation Is Not

Meditation is not about deleting your thoughts and feelings, though it would sometimes be great if we could do that! You'll never stop thoughts and feelings coming into your mind – it's like telling our heart to stop beating. Many shy away from meditating because they think it's a religious practice. Although many religions do use meditation, especially Buddhists and Hindus who do it for spiritual reasons, it is not only a religious practice. Some of the most anti-religious people find immense value in meditating.

What Meditation Is

The simplest explanation of meditation is that it's training you to help notice your thoughts and feelings. Most people don't notice thoughts so they become a part of who we are.

Let's imagine you're driving along a highway and, all of a sudden, another driver swerves in front of you, forcing you to brake heavily. You'll get angry, probably yell something and show them a rude hand gesture. You might think this is a natural reaction but there's an alternative. After the driver swerved, what if you noticed you your mind wanting to get angry but instead of letting the thought cause you to become angry, you choose to let the feeling pass you by. This might sound impossible, but it doesn't take long to become an expert at noticing triggers for your thoughts and emotions and then deciding not to let them affect you.

Isn't it natural to get angry if someone cuts you off in traffic? The Dalai Lama's response suggests otherwise: *"Holding onto anger is like holding onto a hot coal and expecting the other person to get burned, but all that happens is you hurt yourself and the other person does not change."* In the traffic example, the other driver might see your hand reaction and feel a bit guilty, but they cannot change what they did. Although you might feel better after letting them know what they did was wrong, ultimately you're the one who is feeling angry and that's not a nice or helpful feeling to have.

The practice of meditation helps you become centred on the present moment. Indefinite loss, as discussed earlier, means it's easier to get lost in the past, present and future. You might feel anxious about the future and depressed about the past. But the future and the past don't actually exist. The past is only your memories and the future is only your idea of it. Both the past and future are in your head. All that actually exists is what is right now: the present. You cannot change the past and the future is unknown. Even reading the first part of this book is in the past and that's only a thought you have now. What is real is what you're reading right now. You cannot be in the past and future, only in the present.

Meditation helps you focus on what's right in front of you and not to become caught up in your thoughts and feelings about the past and future. You'll still have those thoughts and feelings, and they never go away, but you no longer get caught up in them. Those thoughts can be helpful; it's helpful to think about your wife's scan next week and how you'll get her to and from the hospital, but you don't want to become so caught up in those thoughts that you forget to notice the present. Think of this like a friend being on their phone when you're having a beer together. There's even a word for it, phubbing; snubbing someone you're physically with for your phone and being so focused on all the inflow of data that you forget to notice what's right in front of you: your friend.

How To Meditate
Now that you know *why* meditation will help you, how do you do it? There are many different techniques out there but the basics

are deceptively simple: you sit down and focus on your breathing as best you can.

1) Find a comfortable place to sit. You don't have to cross your legs like a monk. I've never been flexible enough to do this so I sit on a chair. I don't recommend lying down because you might fall asleep, unless you want to use meditation to help you fall asleep, but you can make yourself comfortable with a nice chair.

2) Take a few deep breaths with your eyes open and then gently shut them.

3) Switch to breathing normally and start to focus on all the sounds around you, near and far.

4) Come back and start to focus your attention on your breathing, without changing how you normally breathe.

5) You can count your breaths (one as you inhale, two as you exhale) up to ten, then start again, which can keep you focused as you start to learn.

6) Go for as long as you want. I set a timer on my phone so I don't have to keep checking to see how long I have left and select a calm sound to end the timer.

What Will Happen During Meditation

What you'll find during meditation is that you start thinking, forgetting about your breath, then catch yourself forgetting. This usually does not happen until you've gone down a long rabbit hole of thinking. Noticing when you've lost focus and your thoughts have taken over is the point. Don't get angry with yourself for losing focus because you'll never stop your thoughts and feelings. Not even the most advanced monk can do this.

What you'll find over time is that you get a little better at catching your distraction and returning to the breath before getting caught up in a thought. You'll find you get better at noticing the thoughts and letting them go. You'll notice you're thinking about your wife's scan next week and that you're worried about what it might show. You know she is worried about the scan too and you're worried about what to say to her. But then you realise that the scan is next week, in the future, and all that matters is what is right now. Right now there is no scan and only the time you have with your wife. You can let go of your thoughts and be present, which is one of the best feelings you'll ever have.

I find it quite amusing when I get so caught up in a thought and go down a whole process with that thought before realising I was meant to be focused on my breath instead. I'll be trying to notice my breath and then end up thinking about what I'll eat for dinner, wondering if I have the ingredients and then thinking how I'll go about getting the ingredients I need. I'll then wonder whether it's raining or not and how I'll get to the shops, then about how many calories that meal will have and when I last ate that meal and, well you get the point. It's super easy to go down the rabbit hole. Our minds do this all the time but we often don't give ourselves the space to be aware of them. Meditating creates space in your mind that allows for deeper thoughts to come to the surface.

Getting Started

Like any new skill, getting started with meditation is hard so be prepared. Remember when you learned to drive a car? It took plenty of practice to become good at changing gears, braking smoothly, indicating and checking mirrors, but now all of this is automatic. You don't have to think about any of this and you can even talk to people while driving.

Go in without any expectations when you meditate. Commit the time for the exercise and if it's a terrible experience, give yourself a break. It's part of your learning. If you find that you're thinking the whole time, remind yourself it's normal, and that over time you'll get better at the exercise. Try not to judge yourself just as you don't judge how well you brush your teeth. It's just a job to be done, whether it's easy or hard, pleasant or enjoyable.

Meditation App Recommendations

There are many apps to help you get started with meditation. The one that worked for me is Headspace by Andy Pecombe who is a former monk. In each guided exercise, he explains why meditation is hard and how to manage expectations. The app has specific exercise packs including for anger, depression and anxiety, which you'll probably be feeling. I find the app's tracker helpful because it adds motivation for maintaining the habit streak. Give the free trial a go before committing. There are plenty of other apps you can use such as Insight Timer, Smiling Mind, Omvana, as well as free meditations on YouTube. Choose them based on whether you like the guide's voice, the length of them, or whatever works for you. If you go to the resources section on www.soyourwifehascancer.com, you can download a guided meditation that I take you through.

Keep meditating and building a habit, even if you just sit for one minute every day until you get used to the practice. It will be so different to anything else you've done before.

HABIT 2 - JOURNALING

Why Journal?

The second powerful habit I recommend is journaling removes all the stuff out of your head onto paper or your electronic notebook. What happens if you let all those thoughts and feelings swim around in your head? You'll become overwhelmed. Journaling helps to give your head some space, like meditation. Talking does the same but often there are things you cannot say to people, like that you wish you could leave the situation or you wish it could all be over. Even telling a therapist this can be difficult. But your journal doesn't judge you.

Isn't journaling like your sister's secret diary, or something only women do? I thought this too but realised journaling is equally a masculine exercise. Confronting the fears and thoughts in your brain is much harder than just pushing them down and pretending they aren't there. To do something as difficult as this is only a job for truly heroic carers.

How To Journal – The Tools You Need

Don't think you have to go and buy a specific journaling notebook. Reduce obstacles and make life as easy as possible. There are many ways you can make something seem harder than it actually is and then never do it.

Don't bother with the million and one journaling apps. I use the built in Notes app on my phone and have a separate journal notebook within them. I like to use my phone or laptop because I always have my phone on me and typing is quick on a laptop. There is a template in the resources section of www.soyourwifehascancer. com

How To Journal – What To Do

Alain de Botton, a philosopher and author, writes that the main emotions humans experience are joy, anger, sadness and anxiety. You can structure your journal entry with headings beginning with, "What I'm happy about," "What I'm angry or sad about," and "What I'm worried about". Put bullet points under these headings, because it's quicker and easier than writing full sentences. Sometimes you might only have one bullet point for each heading, or only one word in total, like "Exhausted". Use the headings if you want, or not. You could jot down everything in your head or just list out what happened today.

You might want to write down your purpose and goal to be a champion carer and husband, and what this translates into for your actions for today. Writing down goals has been proven to lead to a far greater chance of achieving them, as opposed to merely thinking about them. When you start doing this, you'll probably start journaling about other aspects of your life such as your health or professional goals.

Nobody is reading your journal except you, so write whatever you want and however much or little you want.

When To Journal

If you're journaling about your feelings and thoughts, the evening is best for this, but journaling any time is better than not at all. If you're journaling for goals, it's best to do this in the morning to set yourself up for the day.

Try to write every day if you can but never put pressure on yourself. You have enough pressure as it is! Journaling is a tool meant to make your life easier, not more stressful. You might write once a week or once a month or only when you feel the need to, or maybe multiple times a day.

This is your journey and your journal, so make it your own. Nobody is judging you or grading you. Keep experimenting and note what is working or not.

HOW TO BUILD A HABIT
AND DEAL WITH RESISTANCE

Let's use the example of journaling. If you think you have to sit down and write a long, five-page journal entry every day, will you do it? No way. If all you need to do is open a new note on your phone and write down one feeling, you've greatly reduced the barrier. Of course you can do this small action every day. And then, after a few weeks, journaling will feel like a normal part of the day. The same goes for meditating: one minute a day is easy to do. After a couple of months, once the habit is installed, you can start increasing the time you meditate because you'll no longer be fighting as much resistance.

The resistance will come because your mind hates change and uncertainty. If you've never journaled before then your mind equates this to going to hunt for a new animal that could potentially kill you. Then your mind will use creative tricks to stop you and return to what is safe and known, telling you that writing down one feeling in a phone note is not real journaling so why bother? Or is one minute of meditating actually helping?

Listen to the voice in your head. Thank it for looking out for you and then get back to the business of being a champion carer. You're building a world-class toolkit to become a world-class carer and husband for this Hero's Journey. No doubt it will be difficult. But after a few months of journaling to notice your feelings and meditating to create space in your day - as well as other methods of coping like seeing a therapist - you'll be in the best place possible to care for yourself and your wife.

EXERCISE: INSTALLING HABITS

Make a list of all the habits you want to install in your life. It could be habits from this part of the book, or it could be anything such as flossing your teeth which is something most people don't do enough.

What's the absolute minimum activity that counts as doing that habit? Write down the minimum viable activity (MVA) down for each habit and exactly when you want to do it, e.g., one minute of meditation or one word in a journal or one tooth for flossing after brushing your teeth.

Put a recurring reminder in your phone to do it. You could ask Siri or Google, *"Every morning at 9am remind me to meditate for one minute."*

Print out the habit tracker from the www.soyourwifehascancer. com website resources section and cross off each day that you do the habit. Then congratulate yourself every time! Your brain loves responding to rewards and gets a dopamine hit.

Don't beat yourself up if you miss a day. Instead try to understand why it happened. Were you tired, or your phone reminder didn't go off, or your wife needed your help at that time? Use this information as learning for the next day: do you need to shift the time the reminder goes off, or reduce the MVA?

Finally, enjoy the power of your brain's autopilot!

4.2

Working
While Caring

*"Most of us spend too much time on what is urgent,
and not enough on what is important."*
— Stephen Covey

Your working life will probably need adjusting. If you're not retired you will need to either remain as the provider for your wife or become the provider if she was the primary income earner. This chapter focuses on how to work while caring for your wife.

Be Upfront With Your Employer About Your Situation
If you're looking for work, and have the flexibility, be upfront with the interviewer that you're a carer and will need to take carers' leave, often at a moment's notice. In this way you can discuss options and the employer's flexibility before you commit to the job. I was upfront in the five or so job interviews I had during the cancer treatment that I was a carer, and was fortunate that all my potential employers were

understanding.

If you already have work, tell your employer as soon as possible what has happened. If they don't understand, you could consider changing jobs, which sounds drastic, but cancer can be extremely unpredictable. If changing jobs is not possible, for example due to a tough job market or your location, you can offer to take leave without pay when you need to care for your wife. You can ask to work flexibly and make up any shortfall in hours taken up visiting doctors, which one of my bosses preferred over continually approving my leave requests.

To raise the conversation with your manager, set aside some time to discuss the situation in person and at length, rather than via email. Email is fine for an initial notice but ask for a meeting, even if you meet over the phone. In the meeting, give your employer the space to ask questions about their concerns and let them know you'll take time to think about solutions if you cannot come up with them at the time. Give your employer a chance to also take the time to process their thoughts once they grasp the enormity of the situation and what it demands of you. Not everyone has been in this situation, so you cannot expect your employer to automatically know what this situation requires of you.

Communicate With Your Boss As Well As Your Team

You've found an understanding employer, or worked out how to address the situation with your current employer? Well done! Now you need to ensure an open line of communication exists. Email your boss if the situation changes to keep them updated and spell out exactly what those changes will mean.

When Natasha started a clinical trial in Sydney, three hours away from our home in Canberra, I gave my boss a brief outline of what the trial would involve, why the trial was so far away, and what changes I would require for my leave requirements. I reminded my boss that I was always a phone call or email away too.

You'll need to communicate openly with others in the organisation and bring them into the loop to help you out. If you have a proactive manager, they can help ensure the workload is spread between your team, so your responsibility is to ensure the team knows what you've been working on. This is especially the case if you suddenly need to take off with a few deadlines coming up. You might feel apprehensive telling people that you are not okay and that you'll need some help, but my experience taught me that so much more good came from opening up rather than pretending everything was okay.

Reduce Your Expenditure

Ultimately, no matter how flexible your employer is, you may need to work fewer hours. This could be an official change to the contract or take the form of leave without pay. Either way, reducing your expenditure is the same as earning more money, and you'll likely need to make some financial sacrifices. Changes can be as small as switching your internet plan from unlimited data to a lesser data allowance, or eating out less often. You might have to make a big change such as downsizing your house so your rent or mortgage expenditure decreases. Moving will be tough but with some planning and help from your mates you can do it without burdening your wife. My friends were only too happy to help me move out of our house after Natasha's diagnosis, and it was a good chance to bond with them.

How much stuff do you buy? You could probably get away with buying less. Happiness lasts longer if it comes from experiences rather than material objects anyway. You'll remember experiences like drives or walks with your wife far more than the stuff you buy her or she buys for you.

Come back to the *why* behind your choice to make sacrifices, which is to spend more time with your wife than at work. It's the right choice, and the only one.

Work Smarter

Working less doesn't always mean producing less work. Many employers now are focused more on work output rather than hours worked, especially after COVID-19 has seen drastic changes for many organisations. They have no reason to complain as long as you get the job done.

Here is some advice to help, though this naturally depends on the type of work you do:

1. **Prioritise**. Your time is limited so make sure you spend it doing work that is both important and urgent before you do the tasks that are not important or that are important but not urgent.

2. **Work super hard** then take breaks where you switch off to rest your mind. I worked in 90-minute blocks where I could not be interrupted except for something important (like a call from my wife or the doctor) and then I took a ten-minute break to stretch my legs. This process allowed me to work and study for an MBA while caring for Natasha and I still work this way now.

3. **Use a calendar app** for all of your tasks, including the deadline for each task. The less you need to remember the better.

4. **Experiment** with working at different times to observe when you're most productive or have the most energy. For me I'm most productive in the morning and for others it's late at night.

5. **Be flexible**. When working from home I could work when Natasha was resting (which was quite often), and then attend

to her needs with full focus knowing I had those other times to work when she rested again.

6. **Run meetings online** rather than in person, if you can. This way you can work from home and still keep in touch with colleagues. Thankfully working online is now more commonplace than ever after COVID-19.

For further reading I recommend the book *Deep Work* by Cal Newport, who explains the necessity of reducing distractions so we can get more done in less time.

Adjust Your Career Goals

You probably need to put your career aspirations on a backburner for now, as difficult as this choice is to accept. That promotion you were working towards is important but is it more important than spending time with your wife and having energy to care for her? Once everything settles down you can always come back to this path. Work can be an escape - it was for me - and this is okay, but decide how hard you now want to work compared to before.

I thought I was taking a step backwards in my career journey after Natasha's diagnosis but, in the end, I was far better off because I could switch my primary focus to Natasha. The experience prepared me to later take on bigger projects than I thought possible. The strength and resilience you gain throughout this journey will prepare you to become an unstoppable force in your career in the future.

You'll be exhausted from your caring duties so following these steps won't always be easy. But learn from mistakes, keep trying, and always do your best. This is all you can ever do, and your best is always more impactful than you think.

4.3

Self-Care

"Taking care of yourself doesn't mean me first, it means me too."
- L.R. Knost

If you wreck yourself by pushing your limits too far, you'll never sustain the focus, energy, motivation and habits that caregiving demands of you. You have to go a little slower to go harder for longer. Being a caregiver is one of the hardest, if not *the* hardest, job you'll ever have so you must look after yourself. This is a marathon not a sprint. Think caring for yourself is selfish? If you don't do it, then you cannot care for your wife. Self-care is vital.

In this chapter I show you how to fuel your body and mind, how to sleep well, and how to take time for yourself. I had no idea how to do this until later in the journey, and when I changed my diet and reliance on sugar and alcohol, life became much easier. Before this I was putting on weight, not exercising, sleeping poorly, overloading my brain, and I later discovered how this all directly impacted my well-being.

The Power Of Sleep

The research on the power of sleep is clear: getting enough high-quality sleep is even more important than diet and exercise for humans to function at their best, yet most people don't get enough. 'Enough' means at least seven to eight hours a night, and high-quality means your mind is able to fully switch off before sleeping so you can enter deep sleep.

Getting enough high-quality sleep is difficult in your situation but at least aim for good-enough rather than perfection. I know how hard this is as I had to sleep on hospital couches and inflatable mattresses. But sleep is when your body rejuvenates all the cells in your body and mind, and you know instinctively that you cannot perform well emotionally, mentally or physically when you don't sleep well. For a great book on the topic, have a look at *Why We Sleep* by Matthew Walker. Here is some advice to follow to help with installing this self-care habit:

- **Practise good sleep hygiene** by trying to sleep at the same time every night when you can. This is difficult with hospital visits and your wife's unpredictable needs but try your best. Set an alarm to remind you when to start preparing for sleep;
- **About an hour before bed, practise a digital sunset routine**, where you turn off anything that could stimulate your mind such as your phone, computer and TV. If you read on an e-book reader then this is fine but try to wear blue-light-blocking glasses if your reader emits light. Blue light tells our brain that the sun is still up even if it isn't, which disrupts our ability to wind down properly;
- **Try to limit the amount of light** on in your house before sleeping and use red lightbulbs after sunset if you can get them, as they eliminate blue light;

- **Try a short wind-down routine**, like a five-minute meditation or a timed breathing exercise. I use one where I lie in bed and breathe in for six, hold for three, breathe out for twelve, hold for three and repeat. There are free recordings you can find on the internet or in apps like Insight Timer to help with this. These exercises help your body come out of fight-or-flight mode by telling it you're relaxed and safe enough to breathe deeply;
- **Try to get outside during the day** so you can get natural light and connect to the circadian rhythm in your body;
- **Take power naps during the day**. If your wife needs to, then this is a good time for you to sleep too.

Again, aim for good enough rather than perfection here. Don't beat yourself up if you look at your phone a few times too close to sleeping and try to take note of when you wake up feeling rested versus exhausted and what you did the night before that might have led to this. Your day actually begins the night before when you're preparing for sleep, so treat this time with importance.

Fuelling Your Body And Mind

How important is high-quality fuel for maximising the performance of your car and tools? Food and drink work the same way for your body and mind. If you're careful about what you consume, then you'll be rewarded with long-lasting energy, focus and emotional control.

As tempting as it will be to go for junk food that feels great in the moment, take a long-term view of what that will do for you. You know the drill. Sugar spikes your energy and then crashes it, as well as causes diabetes and obesity. Processed food such as cheeses pumped with preservatives, processed meats high in salt and refined carbohydrates (for example, white bread and pasta) are also not helpful. Nutritious and fresh foods with vegetables and quality ingredients make us feel good, even if they're not as tasty.

Aim for good enough rather than perfection. It's okay to have pizza, beers and ice cream occasionally, but make them a treat once a week that you look forward to. In the meantime, try to make eating healthily as easy as possible. You could try the following pieces of advice:

- **To avoid meal planning** and so you don't have to think about what to cook or buy, consider using a home-cooking meal service that delivers the ingredients and recipes to your door once a week. They usually have special offers for new customers.
- **If you don't have the energy or time** to cook, prepare in advance when you do. Cook up batches of meals and keep them in the freezer so you can defrost them and eat a healthy meal.
- **To avoid decision fatigue** when deciding what to eat, sign up for a meal-planning service like Mealime (not a typo) or Paprika.
- **Ask someone to help you** by cooking something once a week. Your family and friends will be happy to have something tangible they can help with.
- **If grocery shopping is too time consuming**, but you don't mind cooking, you could ask someone to buy your groceries for you when they shop for theirs, and then transfer them the money. Most large supermarket chains now allow for online grocery shopping and delivery. This might be new to you and a little more expensive but could be well worth the effort. I now find it easy to do and far less time-consuming than walking up and down food aisles;

- **If you want to use a food delivery service**, then try to opt for healthier meals.

Using Alcohol to Cope

A common trap for men is to drink alcohol excessively as a coping mechanism. It's easy to understand why: alcohol helps you relax, takes your mind off burdens, and can taste great.

In the end, though, alcohol is a drug. In small quantities, such as one glass of wine, it's harmless, but often it's tempting to pour another and spiral out of control, especially after one glass or one beer.

The risks of using alcohol are especially high when we take up the position of our wife's carer. What if you're suddenly required to drive her to hospital, but are over the legal limit? What if she suddenly needs some medicine or some particular food but you cannot drive? What if she needs you to talk to a doctor on the phone when she has a pain flare, and you cannot remember what medicines she is on? What if you administer some medicine but give the wrong medicine or dosage? Or what if she wants to spend some quality time with you but you are too drunk to focus?

I love my beer like anyone else, but I made a switch to low- and no-alcohol beers to help me when I wanted the flavour. Thankfully there are now many companies that brew these and are actually pretty good. I'll still occasionally have an alcoholic beer, but I do it to enjoy the particular flavour rather than for the alcohol.

If you notice alcohol is a problem or is a potential problem, talk to your GP and they will give you healthier ways to cope, such as referral to a therapist or antidepressant medication.

Exercise To Elevate Your Mood And Energy

Exercise is vital for mental health and energy management, so it's important to fit this into your schedule. Exercise is a natural method of helping you feel better because of the endorphins released which can last all day. It helps you sleep better and your body's blood and oxygen to flow more freely. You might not have time to exercise daily, especially if life gets hectic at home with your wife's needs, but a small amount of exercise spread throughout the day can help. Any type of movement works, even if it doesn't feel like strenuous exercise.

To help you exercise, you could ask a friend if they could be your exercise buddy. They could come over to your house and go for a walk, run, a round of golf or a bike ride with you on a weekly basis. You needn't be far from your wife and you can still prioritise keeping healthy. You could also go for a walk with your wife if she has the energy. She might be glad to get out of the house or hospital. If she isn't feeling up to it, perhaps she can go out in a wheelchair with you pushing her, something Natasha and I enjoyed.

If being away from your wife is impossible, try a workout programme at home. There are countless apps to help you with this and you don't need to buy equipment. Some, like the seven-minute workout, can be squeezed in when your wife is taking a nap. Another option is to check out some of the free online workouts available on YouTube.

You don't need to be a bodybuilder like Arnold Schwarzenegger or a Formula 1 driver like Lewis Hamilton, but a few sessions a week will give you more energy, help you sleep better and boost your mood, which will in turn help you and help you care for your wife. I took up boxing when I was in the Philippines because it's a popular sport there. This had the benefit of helping me get away from the house for a short time, I had an activity that required all my attention, I could release my anger, and I became fit and strong. I felt physically like a true warrior, which helped me think of the whole journey this way. When I couldn't get away I would use a skipping rope at home or just do some push-ups or walking up and down stairs in the hospital.

Protecting Your Body

An important part of being a champion carer is protecting yourself from injury because the task of caregiving becomes even harder if you injure yourself. If your wife needs help being lifted, ask a physiotherapist for advice, and they can show you how to lift her without damaging yourself or her. Use your legs and core rather than bending your back. A physiotherapist can give you core exercises to strengthen yourself and prevent injury, which can be done indoors without much time required. Some physiotherapists are in hospitals, but you can see one privately if not.

Preventing injury was something I realised too late. The problem was that adrenaline was masking the pain when I was busy lifting Natasha in and out of bed, chairs and cars. This is the job of adrenaline but I was not doing my back any favours at the time. I suffered intense and constant lower back pain which made sitting down and exercise difficult. It took me close to ten months after Natasha passed away to get rid of my back pain. I saw physiotherapists, myotherapists, remedial massage therapists and did a whole heap of strengthening exercises to try to get better. Prevention is better than cure, and I wish I had gotten help earlier in the process.

Letting Anger Out In A Healthy Way
The feeling of anger will become familiar to you on this journey. Try to not let those feelings affect you and those around you. You don't need your temper to get the better of you and cause further strain in your relationship.

I bottled up my anger to avoid scaring others or pushing them away. This was fine, except that by not letting the anger out at all I ended up harming myself with a clenched jaw, excess adrenaline, and tight muscles. There are a few ways you can release anger out in a healthy way that don't jeopardise your relationship with those around you:

- **Write down your feelings**. Pretend you're yelling, but instead you're expressing yourself on your computer, phone or paper;
- **Talk about your feelings** with a mate or doctor;
- **Go to a secluded place** and let your anger out. I like to go out into the bush far away from people, so I don't scare anyone!
- **Scream inside your car** where you won't worry about how loud you are;
- **Scream into a pillow** if you need to release your anger in the moment but cannot leave the house;
- **Sign up for a boxing class** or do some high-intensity activities with someone. In the Philippines, I had a friend who would take me to a shooting range occasionally, which helped because I could just do 'manly', high-intensity activities that left no room for other thoughts;
- **If you enjoy golf**, go send a bucket of poor golf balls down the driving range;
- **Exercise** to let your energy out;
- **Take a deep breath**, notice the anger, and instead of acting on it stop and look inwards at yourself and the emptiness

you feel inside. There will be times when you struggle to contain the anger, and this is okay. Notice the triggers and how the anger affected you as well as those around you. Think about ways you can try reacting differently next time.

Take Time For Yourself
Spend time doing things you enjoy, with people you like, free from guilt. Of all the self-care activities you can do, it's crucial you make time to focus on you. Yes, you are your wife's primary carer but is it true you're the only person in the world who must care for her every minute of every day? Most likely not, even if you are her favourite carer or the carer who is most familiar with her needs.

Talk about this with your wife. Let her know you need some time off, and that you'll work out how someone can be with her if she needs that. Some advice to get started with this:

- **Ask your wife** what friend or family member she would like to come and look after her while you're gone, and this can double as time for her to spend with a friend or relative she is missing;
- **If no-one is around**, then look up whether there are respite nurses who can come in for some time, or can take your wife into a hospice for the day;
- **Talk to your wife about what you would like to do** with your time. If she doesn't want you to go, then try to push back and say that if you don't take this time off you won't survive the marathon with this level of emotional and physical energy expenditure. She might not understand until she sees you come back after a morning or day or weekend off and how rejuvenated and present you are, so ask her to at least let you try it before judging.

Even towards the end, when Natasha was needing the most intensive care, she pushed me to step out and do something good for myself. There were respite nurses in Canberra who were able to look after her and who pushed me to take a break, because they sensed I was both physically and emotionally exhausted. I would go out and get a coffee, take a boxing class, get a nice lunch, or go go-karting with some mates. I always had my phone on me if there was an emergency, and eventually I learned to enjoy the time without feeling guilty.

With all these self-care exercises, try them and see what works or doesn't work. Experiment with your own. Only you will know what works best for you, so treat everything like a learning exercise. Putting yourself first will seem strange, but if you don't care for yourself you cannot care for your wife.

KEY POINTS FROM PART 4

- It might seem selfish to focus on yourself, but if you're not coping well, you cannot be the champion carer and husband your wife needs.

- Creating habits will help you make difficult, crucial tasks easier to implement. Use habits to run these tasks on autopilot: tasks like meditation and journaling which might be new and strange, but after a while it will instead seem strange not to do them.

- Your work will be affected by this journey, but you don't have to stop working. If you're open and honest with your boss and colleagues, you can work out creative solutions. These include working less, working from home, working smarter instead of harder and adjusting your career goals. Work will always be there. You'll come out of this journey stronger than ever before, so have the courage to take a step back for now to focus on the most important job you have, caring for your wife.

- There are a number of changes to implement in your life that will help you last for the marathon, including eating well, exercising, sleeping well, not relying on drugs like alcohol, releasing anger in a safe and healthy manner, and taking time out for yourself.

PART FIVE

YOUR WIFE'S TREATMENT AND CARE

In this part you'll learn all about your wife's treatment, interacting with her doctors, planning techniques and tools to care for her at home.

5.1

Cancer Treatment Options

This chapter looks at the treatment your wife could undergo at different stages of her journey, including surgery, chemotherapy and radiotherapy. I focus on the partner's experience of the treatments and where you can intervene, rather than specifics about the treatments. Every patient has a unique situation and this is not medical advice. Your wife's doctors will give you specific information, and cancer treatments are continually updated with the latest research. For example, there were cancer trials available three years after Natasha was diagnosed that were not available at the time of diagnosis. Given this, use the following advice as a framework for approaching any kind of treatment.

SURGERY

Modern society is blessed with extremely precise medical knowledge and procedures. It's rare for surgery to go wrong, and we now have whole teams of people involved: the anaesthetist, surgeons, nurses, assistants, and all the hospital personnel. Although the idea of surgery can be scary, it's reassuring to know z

Before Surgery

Your job at this stage is to help your wife choose a surgeon and to talk with them about what surgery will entail to help you both make an informed decision.

The first step is to help your wife with choosing a surgeon, if this is an option. Research shows cancer outcomes, for patients with some cancers, are better if you have a surgeon who has experience in that particular type of cancer surgery, rather than a general surgeon. It might not be possible to find a specialist cancer surgeon where you live but try your best either by asking around in the hospital nearest to you or travelling to another hospital.

Once you've chosen a surgeon, try to attend all the appointments with your wife so you can be there to ask questions and wrap your head around the procedure too. This will make the process much less frightening, and you can be there to support your wife.

You can help by listening to your wife when she voices her concerns. If there are difficult decisions to be made about treatment (for example, the order of treatment, or alternatives for treatment), you can request to have her case discussed at a multidisciplinary meeting, where surgeons, internal medicine physicians, as well as medical and radiation oncologists all attend and provide a recommendation for the path going forward.

Assuming your wife has made the decision to go ahead with surgery, try to make sure she doesn't have to worry about anything except the procedure. On the day, pack your wife's clothes and toiletries for the hospital and generally take control of the process of getting her to hospital. Doing this for Natasha helped her to focus solely on the draining task of getting showered and dressed. It helped her feel looked after.

During surgery

At this point your only job is to wait and take some time for yourself. Once your wife is wheeled into the operating theatre there won't be much you can do. I recommend you hang around in the waiting area in case she comes out early or if the doctors need to talk to you. You can read a book, get work done or take some time to relax and re-group. This is a rare time without your wife and you can spend it sitting with your own thoughts and feelings or praying if that works for you. I felt apprehensive during this time but was still largely in shock that this was even happening at all. Having the time to just sit with my thoughts helped to process some of my thoughts and feelings.

You can ask the surgeon if it's okay to look at the tumour once they have removed it if you're feeling up to it and if the surgeon allows it. This can give you a sense of what you are up against in the journey to come. I didn't think this was possible until Natasha's surgeon made the offer for us to look at the tumour. I remember staring at the tumour for a long time, in disbelief that it had been growing inside my wife silently for potentially up to a decade.

Immediately After Surgery

At this stage your job will be to ensure your wife is comfortable and has enough pain relief. It is also to be there for her and give here a sense of love and stability when everything seems so out of control.

Immediately after surgery your wife will be tired from the anaesthetic and painkillers because her body has experienced a shock and is working out how to deal with that shock. She will stay in hospital for a few days for monitoring so make her as comfortable as possible. Bring her flowers to put beside her hospital bed and enjoy spending time with her. Keep reminding her how proud you are of her for her strength and for doing something so major.

Sufficient pain relief is important. Your wife may experience pain flares as the painkillers wear off. If this happens, call the nurses immediately before the pain gets any worse. Try to get on top of it as quickly as you can. Call the nurses often, especially if your wife's pain tolerance is typically low. If the nurses are not willing or able to give effective pain relief (for instance because the last dose wasn't long ago), ask if they or you can speak to the doctors about it.

In the days and weeks after surgery keep monitoring your wife's pain levels, ensure she always has enough pain medication available, make her comfortable, and do everything you can so all she needs to focus on is resting.

CHEMOTHERAPY

Not everyone will need chemotherapy, nor will it be suitable or recommended for all patients. Chemotherapy, or chemo, is the name of medication used to fight cancer and although it can seem scary, everyone has a unique experience. The dosages are tailored to your wife and account for many aspects, including her age and overall health. Getting your wife through her chemotherapy sessions is one task where you can be helpful as her husband.

Here again you'll often feel helpless but there is still much within your control. Helping your wife be comfortable and manage her symptoms before, during and after chemo is within your control.

Before Chemo

Chemotherapy drugs are changing all the time so your job at this stage is to find out as much information as you can about the particular drug or drug combination your wife will take. Check whatever you've heard about other people's experience of chemotherapy with your wife's oncologist, because they can explain everything and account for your goals and lifestyle as a couple.

Be clear on the aim of treatment so you're fully aware of, and happy with, the goals of chemo. Is the chemo curative or palliative (just for pain relief)? Ask questions on the magnitude of the benefit of chemotherapy and expected side effects for your wife, as well as how to manage those side effects and who to contact if they are not manageable at home.

- **Talk to your wife's oncologist.** They will tell you what all the possible side effects are and how to best manage them. Some drugs can have a huge number of side effects while others are hardly noticeable, and your wife's oncologist will tell you which are most likely for her. All drugs have side effects as this is the nature of adding something foreign to the body. They attempt to do something the body cannot do on its own, so the body may not function normally with drugs in the system.
- **Research credible sources online.** This can sometimes be more helpful than the oncologist's information because you can take your time to read about the drugs. The most reliable sources for information are found from established organisations such as eviQ, the Cancer Council in Australia and Cancer Research UK. You can search for their websites easily online. These are advised because there is often too much information provided by drug company websites, blogs, forums and online/social media groups. If you do look at these, know that someone else's experience with the drug will almost definitely be different to your wife's. No two people will have the same medical conditions or cancer biology. Even cancers of the same site and

cell origin have different driving mutations and inherent biologies. No two people will be the same age, race, sex, fitness level, have the same mental coping ability, have necessarily had the same drugs to treat it in the past, or have the same diet as your wife. This is something you should tell your wife too because she might be reading everything she can.

During Chemo
Chemotherapy can be delivered in different ways, most commonly through an intravenous drip directly into the veins or orally with a tablet. Even each of these methods can be done differently, either for a short or long duration; in hospital or at home; or a combination of these.

You have three main jobs during this stage:
1. Plan ahead to anticipate, manage and avoid issues;
2. Make a medication list;
3. Communicate and be flexible.

Plan ahead: You'll need to plan ahead based on her schedule so you can take the time needed to be with your wife during her chemo. Each chemo session is an experiment to see what works and doesn't work, so you can be more prepared for the next one. One would expect the same type of side effects with each cycle/dose of the same regimen. It's therefore important to note and tell your wife's oncologist about all the side effects so these can be anticipated, managed and possibly avoided altogether in the next cycle.

Luckily, I was able to work from the hospital and was allowed to sleep in the same room when Natasha had the longer intensive chemo sessions. The best type of chemo Natasha had was a small dose of tablets, which she could take anywhere we went and didn't need to be administered in hospital.

Make a medication list: Write down which medication your wife is on at any given time as well as the dosage. Sometimes, in the heat of the moment, you could panic and forget the precise name of the drug or get confused with a drug she might have been on in the past. If you have to go to an emergency room if the side effects are particularly difficult to manage, the doctors will need to know exactly what she is taking so they can ensure the other medication they give doesn't react negatively with this. I will give you some tools in chapter 5.3 that you can use to easily track medication.

Communicate and be flexible: Communication is vital, and this is something covered all throughout this book. Sometimes your wife might want to appear to be dealing with the drug without an issue and she might hide her struggles. Without being pushy, keep asking her how she is coping and what you can do to help make her more comfortable. Your wife might develop strange food cravings or food intolerances due to her hormones being messed with, so be prepared to be flexible.

For Natasha, we would have supplies of random food on standby, such as plain ice-cream cones with no ice-cream! Her sense of smell was also affected, and some foods she normally loved would smell disgusting to her during chemo, so we had to keep those well away. These reactions will be unique to your wife's experience, so the drug manufacturers and oncologists cannot tell you beforehand what will happen.

During Chemo Breaks

Chemo regimens often have an intense "on" period as the drugs fight to get rid of the cancer and then a break for the body to recover before the next "on" period. If you're lucky there might be a couple of days before the next "on" period where your wife is fully rested and has her normal energy back. During chemo breaks your only job is to make the most of these days of normal energy!

If you feel like all you're doing is waiting for the next chemo session, then you'll quickly feel helpless and trapped. Take her out to lunch or a movie or do something you both enjoy. This is important for helping you feel like a normal couple and giving you both something to look forward to. You must try to feel in control, even if for a short amount of time, and you can have more control over what you do as a couple when she is feeling okay.

Depending on the medication and dosage, your wife will be exhausted when recovering. Look after her well in this time. Bring her food in bed and re-think what activities you can do together that don't require much energy. If you both like board games you could play those and bring them into the hospital if she has a longer stay there. Natasha and I ended up watching the whole five seasons of *Downton Abbey*, a British historical drama series, during chemo breaks! It was easy to enjoy and a great escape from the world we were living in.

If you want to go on a drive, try to plan ahead for rest breaks in case your wife became nauseous or wants fresh air. We soon got to know where to find clean toilets! Always make sure you know where the nearest hospital is in case of emergency.

Taking A Long Break From Chemo

Taking a long break from chemo might seem strange but a big part of a cancer battle is making the most of quality of life rather than only using anti-cancer drugs. Some oncologists will want to go from one chemo regimen to the next without a break because they feel pressure from the patient and their family to keep doing something. But it might be worth considering this option if the chemo has a negative impact on quality of life while only having a negligible impact on the cancer.

Discuss this carefully as a couple and with your wife's oncologist. You can ask them whether a break would be suitable or not, knowing that - in many situations - it won't be. For curative-intent patients, where the aim of chemo is to fight the chemo, unnecessary breaks in treatments can be harmful and reduce the effectiveness of treatment. Although a few days may not make a difference, weeks or months of delay is not recommended for most curative cancer treatments. However, there are some slow-growing cancers where months of delay is unlikely to be harmful, such as low-grade lymphomas.

Halfway through Natasha's cancer journey, her oncologist wanted to give her a break from chemo. He explained that the cancer was not growing aggressively and wanted to compare the cancer's growth to growth without the chemo. If there was not a substantial difference between having chemo or not, then he reasoned there was no point making Natasha sicker from having chemo. At first, listening to his advice felt like we were giving up and not doing anything for her anymore. But we *were* fighting the cancer, only with a longer-term perspective. It was the same as an army taking a break to build up strength and decide on a new strategy, rather than being in combat all the time.

The oncologist assured us the time off would allow Natasha's body to build up strength as well as give her a much-needed break for a few months to feel normal and do normal activities. Natasha ended up feeling okay enough to travel, and we booked an overseas trip to Israel and England. We also took a few road trips within Australia. Eventually, there was a clinical trial suitable for her condition and she decided to enrol in one. She coped much better during the trial because her body had built up some strength and she was feeling better psychologically.

Ultimately the decision to take a long break directly affects your wife, so she will have the final say. One question you could ask your wife's oncologist is what they would do if this was their daughter or sister, or themselves. Many bristle at this question, because they know first-hand how tough the cancer journey is and don't want to think about it happening to them. One oncologist took a week to think about her answer, which was the same amount of time she gave us to think about a new regimen. She then told us she would have decided differently from Natasha, but she understood where Natasha was coming from and fully supported her decision.

Radiation Therapy
Radiation therapy targets a particular anatomical area of the body with high doses of radiation to kill cancer cells and shrink tumours. Radiation is more similar to surgery than systemic therapies such as chemotherapy and immunotherapy. It can replace or supplement these treatments. There are different types of radiation treatment, some super precise and others that target a broader area. If you want to find out more about radiotherapy, Canberra Hospital has a 14-minute patient information video you can find by searching for "YouTube, radiotherapy, Canberra hospital". This video explains radiation therapy clearly and other hospitals have made similar videos.

Before Radiation

As before with chemo, your job here is to help your wife prepare for treatment by meeting with doctors and helping her get to and from the hospital. Before the treatment begins, if radiation is targeted at the head, neck or upper chest, a plastic mesh mask will be made to fit your wife that keeps her head in the precise one spot during the treatment. If radiation is done on other areas of the body, the therapists may use immobilisation devices such as head or knee supports, a board with handles to hold onto (wing board or breast board), or a vacuum bag that is individually shaped to your wife. During the planning scan and radiation treatment your wife will need to be undressed in the area to be treated and then dressed in a supplied gown, and you can help her with this if she is in pain.

During Radiation

On the day of treatment your wife will need to change into a gown and then lie on a bench while the therapists administer the therapy. The bench is solid and uncomfortable, but if your wife needs a break the therapists can pause the treatment, let her stretch, then continue. You can plan for any pain flares by reminding or helping your wife to take pain relief beforehand.

Because of the low dose, but potentially harmful, radiation levels in the room while the machine is on, no one except the patient can stay in the room. The radiation therapists go to a room to the side of the treatment room. There will be window into the treatment room with a window and they will use a microphone to speak with your wife during the treatment.

When Natasha was in a lot of pain, I became an expert at lifting her in and out of her wheelchair. I asked if I could wheel her into the radiation room, lift her onto the bench and then lift her off when the treatment was over. The therapists were happy to allow this, and I felt good to be involved in this way, but each hospital will have its own practices and procedures so don't expect to be able to do this.

After Radiation

Following radiation your job is to help your wife with anything she needs and to keep her comfortable. For the vast majority of patients who have external beam radiotherapy or high-dose-rate brachytherapy (internal radiation treatment), radiation only goes through the body while the machine is on, and your wife is not radioactive after treatment.

Like the other treatments, there may be side effects, depending on where the radiation is targeted. There are patient information sheets on possible side effects for your wife's particular cancer which you can find online such as the eviQ website. Although you or your wife might be tempted to read internet forums about others' experience of radiation, assure your wife that her experience will be unique. She mightn't have any side effects. However, you can probably expect her to be quite tired afterwards because her body is getting a lot thrown at it on top of the stress of going to and from hospital. Help her relax and rest, and make sure you're prepared if the side effects do come into play.

CLINICAL TRIALS

A clinical trial in humans takes place when first experiments show some promising outcomes. Have you seen footage of scientists testing medicines on animals or in other ways in a laboratory? It's one thing to be effective in a rat but another in humans. If the trial treatment gets to the point of human testing, you can be certain it was safe and effective in the lab before this. The fundamental reason for a clinical trial is the variability of human beings in their illnesses and in their reactions to them. A trial considers whether the treatment is safe and effective.

Trials of new treatments might not take place if your wife has a common cancer that has had plenty of research done already, or there might not be enough interested clinicians, funding or clinical trial support staff.

The trial goes through a number of phases, from a small group of people mainly looking at the safety and side effects, gradually building up to more people and without a placebo. After the treatment has been shown to be safe and effective, it becomes mainstream. Your wife might be given a placebo, which is a pill that tastes and looks like the real one but is used to compare the effectiveness of the actual drug to the fake one. If a trial has a placebo control, you won't be told which is which, but if the trial is beyond this stage, which Natasha's was, they will tell you that all patients are on the real drug.

What Happens If Your Wife Is Offered A Clinical Trial

At some point during your wife's journey, her doctors might suggest she takes part in a clinical trial. When Natasha and I first heard this, we were scared. We had no idea what a trial was, and the sound of it made us think of rats in a lab. Would it be safe? What were other patients' reactions to it? How would it work? These are typical questions. Your wife's doctor can answer all these questions and more if the discussion takes place.

If your wife is offered a clinical trial and decides to enrol, she will not only potentially be benefitting from the latest research but also will contribute to research for future patients. The trials will have been approved by an ethics committee and the aim of the trial should always be to improve outcomes (either better cancer control or less side effects for the same cancer control).

There is always more intensive monitoring than what is the case in standard practice. There may be more forms to fill out and more tests as well as appointments.

Note that clinical trials might run in many different cities, and you should express to your wife's doctor an interest in being involved even if you need to travel as they may not have thought of referring her. Natasha's trial was in Sydney, three hours' drive away, but we were desperate to try something new as at this point Natasha had exhausted all available chemotherapy options. Often, drug companies foot the bill for travel, so feel free to ask about this too. The drug company running Natasha's clinical trial paid for all the medications and the transport expenses to Sydney. The drug company has an interest for the trial to be positive after all.

Ask Questions

You've had so much practice with asking questions that asking more shouldn't phase you by now. Build your list of questions and then run through them with the doctor, putting aside any fear of sounding stupid so you can focus on gathering all the information you need. The doctor will answer all of them and if you're not happy with some of the answers, such as if there are bad side effects, you can ask for some time to decide, discuss with your wife and do your own research in this time.

Do Your Research

For each stage of the trial, the drug companies have information online and in brochures you can get from your wife's doctor on the drugs. However, the doctors cannot tell you how other patients are coping on the drug. This information might affect the trial's validity because you might think your wife has those symptoms as well when she in fact does not.

During The Trial
Use all the tools you develop throughout this book - like planning, record-keeping and communication - to make the trial as straight-forward as possible.

Your wife's oncologist may give you their mobile number and email address, especially if your wife is on a trial or at least so that you can contact the assistant researcher. Natasha's oncologist and the research assistant offered their mobile numbers and I would call them whenever I needed help understanding the side effects or with any questions that we had.

IMMUNOTHERAPY

Immunotherapy is a newer form of treatment that aims to build up the immune system to fight the cancer from within. Although this treatment seems like a silver bullet, at the moment it's still in early stages of development. It's only available for certain types of cancer and is a rapidly changing field. The best person to check with will be your wife's oncologist rather than doing research online. If you do want to read anything online, you can check out the patient information sheets specific to the immunotherapy regimen (drug, dose, interval) by searching for the eviQ website.

ALTERNATIVE TREATMENTS

What Are They?
Alternative treatments are anything other than the treatments discussed above. When looking at these, I recommend reading the website of the world-famous Sloan Kettering Cancer Centre (www.mskcc.org/research/ski) as this covers alternative therapies including acupuncture, herbs and supplements. They have an app you can download from their website.

Who To Talk To About Alternative Treatments

If you're interested in trying alternative treatments, discuss them with your wife's oncologist first. If your wife is on any of the conventional treatments discussed above, or needs to be at a later point, then alternative therapies may interact negatively with this.

If your wife is not on active treatment, alternative therapies can be considered. Many oncologists won't have specific training in administering alternative treatments, however, so to find out more you can talk directly with practitioners. When meeting with them, apply the same techniques you learned earlier about choosing a doctor and working with them.

What To Be Aware Of With Alternative Treatments

Be deeply sceptical of any alternative practitioner who suggests your wife doesn't require recommended conventional medical management.

Some experimental treatments can be heavily charged and inaccurately advertised. There are people who have claimed to heal their cancer without any use of the formal medical system. It's disappointing there are people who want to make financial gains in providing false hope to patients.

DOING RESEARCH ON YOUR WIFE'S CANCER AND TREATMENT

Everyone is unique. Your wife has unique genes, a unique diet, history, circumstances, and a unique husband. It's impossible to look at another person's experience with treatments and conclude your wife will have the same experience.

Ultimately, the best source will always be your wife's doctors and pharmacists. They can give you all the information you need on side effects of medicines as well as what to expect with certain treatments. They have done many years of training to get where they are and their information only comes from scientific research rather than from unfounded opinions. They see so many patients that they can give you a doctor's insight into the common side effects their patients suffer as opposed to you and your wife having to research individual stories.

Even oncologists don't have a crystal ball. Some patients do much, much better than the average. It may be useful to ask for the best-case and worst-case scenario. Plan for the worst and hope for the best.

Aside from your wife's doctors, there are many reliable sources of information available. The go-to place for information today is online where there is plenty of excellent information but some sources can be misleading and sub-par.

Websites That Use Academic Research

Organisations such as eviQ, Cancer Council and Cancer Research UK base their recommendations on research and have checked that research for any issues. After your wife's oncologist, these sources are the most recommended due to their accessibility and accuracy.

Many people shy away from academic research and favour an opinion online instead. Academic research takes that opinion as a hypothesis and then rigorously tests the hypothesis with as many real patients as possible. Then these conclusions are tested by multiple researchers to make sure nothing was missed in the experiments. This will always be far more reliable than one person's opinion on the internet. The whole reason we have advanced medicine now is due to this scientific approach to research. You can ask your wife's oncologist for the research on a particular drug, which they should be more than happy to give to you.

Academic research cannot cover every single scenario. For example, colorectal cancer used to typically only occur in older people so not much research has been done on how it affects younger people. When Natasha was diagnosed at 28 years old, not one doctor could give a clear prognosis as they didn't have the research on it.

Drug Company Websites
Most drug companies will have a website for the drug or drugs your wife is on. You might think they would try to hide side effects to make their drug seem better than it is, but it's actually the opposite. The company has an interest in covering itself for every possibility so they will list all side effects they found in people when testing the drug, even if they only happened in one patient in the trial. This can be a problem because it's easy to become overwhelmed by the information rather than having it distilled and personalised by your wife's oncologist.

Be Wary When Researching Online
Forums are brilliant places for people all over the world to share ideas, but they can be troublesome. Few are moderated, and there might be nasty comments there, especially if a cancer patient is having a tough time or feels strongly about their beliefs. You and your wife don't need to expose yourself to that sort of energy.

Always do the research to back up opinions you come across or ask your wife's oncologist. Forums are full of people's individual opinions and not every cancer patient has a medical background. Just because someone has an opinion that chemotherapy is not as good as natural therapies doesn't mean they are correct.

Someone who had a tough time doing radiation treatment and has written all about it on their blog doesn't mean your wife will have the same experience.

CONCLUSION

This chapter has discussed many of the treatments available for cancer. Everyone is different so what is offered to your wife will be unique to her circumstances. For some patients there won't be any suitable treatment, in which case there are other options that include management of symptoms to reduce pain.

By now you have an arsenal of tools to help you approach these options confidently and with the mindset of learning all the time. The key in all of this is to rely heavily on your wife's doctors as her experts, which we explore in the next chapter, as well as listening to your and your wife's intuition, judgement or advice.

5.2

Doctors

There will be many people travelling with you during this journey so bring them along with you and get along with them to make the journey easier for all. Being an heroic carer for your wife is not so much about mastering big difficulties but becoming comfortable with many small aspects that, when combined, make the whole journey that much easier.

You'll interact regularly with your wife's doctors and they will come to know you and your wife intimately. Illness is deeply personal, and much will need be revealed to doctors for them to do their job in deciding the most appropriate treatments.

In this chapter I help you choose a doctor, learn how to treat them well, and discover how to coordinate all of them to ensure the best possible outcome. When I refer to doctors in this chapter, I mean anyone who is responsible for helping your wife, including general practitioners, your family doctor or primary-care physician, surgeons, and oncologists.

Choosing your wife's doctors

Hopefully, you've not had to experience dealing with cancer specialists before this, so you may be in the dark as to what makes a good doctor. I was. You might not get the chance to choose your wife's doctor, depending on the health system you're in, but if you can, here is some advice for finding doctors that suit you both:

- Find a doctor who you can tell genuinely cares about their job and your wife;
- Ask yourself if you feel listened to by the doctor. Do you feel comfortable with them? Professional treatment is crucial but cancer affects a person's whole life and it's helpful if you can get along well with your wife's doctors;
- Meet with a few doctors if you have the option;
- Ask them about their approach to treatment, for example, are they open to giving breaks if they enhance quality of life or do they want to do as much treatment as possible?
- Have they listened to and considered what you both want? Having treatment is always the patient's choice and the decision should not affect the relationship with your wife's doctor, whether or not they agree with your choice.

You and your wife always have the final say on treatment. If you don't like the oncologist's approach, you can try finding a new one depending on the system in your country. In Australia, you don't require an oncologist's permission to seek another opinion. You can ask to see a different oncologist in the public health system although it's easier to change oncologists in the private system. An oncologist should be able to explain the treatment recommendations and the reasons for them, all possible alternatives, including no treatment, and the pros and cons of each option.

Regardless of your choice, they should be able to support you and care for you. If you do wish to see another one, options include asking your wife's oncologist for a second opinion or asking the referring doctor to refer your wife to a different oncologist.

Make a good connection with your health professionals
No nurse or doctor will ever admit it, but I believe that if they like their patient they will do more than they usually would to ensure the best possible treatment for that patient. After all, they're only human and you only need to think about how you respond to your own customers, students, bosses and colleagues who treat you nicely. The best part is this doesn't take that much effort. Some advice:

- Smile at your doctors, nurses and the receptionist when you come in for your appointment. There will be times you don't feel like smiling but try if you can. They are there to help you;
- Remember the names of your wife's doctors and nurses, if you can, or at least use their name if they have a name badge. You could write the names down in a notebook. Dale Carnegie in his timeless book *How to win friends and influence people* spends a whole chapter on the importance of using a person's name because it's the essence of our identity and builds a deep connection. Never be afraid to ask for someone's name if you've forgotten it. In your situation people know you have much on your mind and will be pleasantly surprised you care enough to ask;
- Thank the doctors and nurses when your appointment is over. It will be natural to get caught up thinking about whether your wife is okay and what comes next, so nobody will be offended if you forget to say this. Simple manners go a long way;
- Bring in some chocolates occasionally for the doctors and

nurses as a small gift. The gifts don't have to be expensive but it's an easy way to show your gratitude;

- Ask them how they are and questions like how long they have been working at the hospital. As always, make sure you genuinely care about them rather than asking for the sake of making small talk;

- Share how you're coping or not coping. Vulnerability is a powerful method of connection, and doctors and nurses will always be understanding. Even if you want to share that you've had a tough week, they can point you in the direction of some useful resources like counsellors at the hospital or organisations to help;

- Try to hold back your anger if something goes wrong. Everyone is doing their best, and hospitals are some of the most complex organisations on the planet. If something doesn't go quite right you might get angry, which is part of your protective mechanism kicking in. If you notice this happening, try to take a few deep breaths. Ask yourself if it will be useful to get angry, or whether you are trying to feel better in the moment. Most of the time anger is not useful and could harm the good relationship you have with her doctors and nurses. The meditation practices discussed in chapter 4.1 will help you master your emotions to notice when you start to get angry, and then let that emotion go;

- Notice if you haven't had enough sleep, which is common, and realise that in this situation your emotions will be triggered more easily. Just noticing this is often enough to then let go of those emotions or to hold back a bit if you feel a certain way;

- Have a friendly and personable approach when communicating with her doctors and nurses. I would start with 'sorry to bother you...' when contacting them or their receptionists to show that I know they are busy with multiple patients and Natasha was not the only person important to them. They almost always replied with 'sure, go ahead' but it's a powerful line to start with. You can find what works and is comfortable for you.

Natasha was truly an expert at this. She genuinely cared about every one of her doctors and nurses. This came from a deep feeling of gratitude for the help they gave her rather than feeling like they were obligated to provide her a service because it was their job.

During the spare time I had when Natasha was resting in the hospital, I would often wander around the hallways to help process my emotions, thoughts, and take my mind off the situation. When I heard patients yelling at the nurses and doctors, though, I felt sad. I couldn't blame them. They were dealing with cancer and had every reason to be upset with what is happening. But as we have discussed, you have the choice with how you respond to your feelings and those around you, even if there is so much out of your control. Being nice instead of angry is by far the harder choice but will always be the best one. This journey was never going to be easy, although small adjustments like the ones suggested in this chapter will make it all a bit more comfortable.

Coordinating Her Doctors: What It Means And Why It's Necessary

The burden of coordinating a patients' doctors usually falls on the carer, and this adds an extra level of anxiety and complexity to the role. You'll find yourself performing this vital role and there are methods you can put in place to make the job easier.

Preparation will make your life easier, especially in emergencies. In non-emergency situations, taking the burden off your wife will help her focus on her health and resting. Often she won't realise all you're doing behind the scenes, but when everything falls into place she will be grateful. It's like how we can take a computer for granted because most people don't understand their inner workings - they just work and we become used to that, but that doesn't mean we aren't grateful for what they do for us.

To coordinate doctors includes:

- Booking appointments to line up with your wife's other schedules, your work schedule, and with all her other appointments. These need to happen in the correct order (for example, blood tests and scans before seeing the oncologist);
- Ensuring your wife has all the necessary medicine prescriptions before she runs out of her current script, which means booking appointments with your wife's doctor before this happens;
- Cancelling appointments when she is too sick to attend them;
- Calling and emailing doctors to seek advice if there are complications;
- Ensuring all doctors know of the other doctors she has, and helping to ensure they are on the same page;
- Ensuring all doctors are up to date with the latest developments.

This sounds overwhelming but with the following strategies you can make life a bit easier for you and your wife.

Engage The Nurse Coordinator's Help
Ask if the hospital has a cancer nurse coordinator to help coordinate and act as a single port of call. This was not offered to Natasha and me, but larger hospitals do have these and will make the following steps much easier.

Enter All Phone Numbers And Email Addresses In Your Phone Or Notebook So You Can Easily Search For Them

The couple of minutes it takes in that moment to enter details into your phone contacts will be a blessing when you're suddenly stressed looking for a number and cannot find the business card or note you saved. You might think you can find this information easily at home, but you're not always home and - in an emergency - you'll at least always have your phone and can easily search for the doctor you need. Do this as soon as you get a phone number from a doctor, especially if they give you their mobile and email address, which not all of them will so don't expect them to. If you cannot remember their name, use a reference like 'Hospital radiation oncologist'.

Use Text Messages

Use text messages to communicate with your wife's doctor if you have their mobile number, which saves you interrupting them in a meeting. They can reply when they are free. A text lets them know why you're reaching out so they can judge whether your news or question is urgent or not. Sometimes you can text something non-urgent like an update, so it doesn't take much of their time or yours, but ensures they know what is happening.

This strategy was helpful when I would have to take Natasha to the emergency room at midnight, which happened a few times due to side effects of the chemotherapy and radiation, and I wanted to update her oncologists without waking them. I could communicate with the doctors while still being next to Natasha, without distressing her by talking on the phone. Sometimes a doctor would call me back after a text if they thought it necessary.

Use Email

Email is another good option for communicating with doctors. Most doctors are more comfortable giving you their email address because they can choose when they open it, and there is not the risk of all their patients endlessly calling them. You can also go into more detail in the email than over text. I would often email Natasha's general practitioner, medical and radiation oncologist all at once so they all received exactly the same message. They would then 'reply-all' so everyone could see the follow-up advice. This was especially useful when Natasha's treatment options became complex towards the end and careful decisions involving many doctors needed to take place. Doctors have many patients and your wife is not the only one, so don't expect them to take half an hour to read an essay you've written in email! Keep it succinct and to the point and, if they need more information they can call or email you, or ask you to set an appointment.

Give Your Contact Information To All The Doctors

I always gave my own contact details to every doctor, even though they had Natasha' details. I found that the doctors would often call me rather than Natasha because they didn't want to disturb her. It was just as easy for doctors to talk to me because I knew everything about her treatment and side effects intimately. You'll generally have more energy than your wife to speak and think clearly about what needs to happen. Sometimes your wife's doctor will want to ask for updates about you, so giving them your number helps them do this easily and privately.

Attend All Appointments If You Can

If you're not there it's harder to know what's happening, and you cannot hold your wife's hand when she needs you. It's vital you're there to contribute your own observations about your wife's reactions, which she might have forgotten. You can remember things the doctor says that she might not have the energy or capacity to remember.

I recognise there are many good reasons for not being able to attend the appointment, whether it's your own illness or surgery, sick or handicapped children/grandchildren. Maybe you don't have sick leave or you're at risk of losing your employment and are without a financial and maybe social welfare safety net. If this is the case, try to ensure someone can go with your wife and take notes, and give that person notes on what you want them to say.

I heard horrible stories from doctors about how some carers would make the patient go to the hospital alone in a taxi because they were too busy at work or they were afraid of hospitals. If you cannot make an appointment, try your best to reschedule it because, whether you like it or not, you're the only person who is able to fully coordinate every single doctor your wife has, and attending appointments is a valuable contribution to your wife's care and your marriage.

You can already see how vital your role is in caring for your wife despite the feelings of helplessness. Focusing on what you can control which, as this chapter has shown is plenty, is essential for everyone involved for you. It's a great boost to your self-esteem and to your wife's appreciation of what you're doing for her.

EXERCISE: CHOOSING AND COORDINATING DOCTORS

What traits are important in doctors to you and your wife? Have you discussed this? If you have a doctor already and they are working out, what is it that you like about them? This is useful to think about if you need a new doctor down the track.

- What are some strategies you can use to build rapport next time you see a doctor or nurse?

- What strategies will you use to coordinate your wife's specialists?

- How do you feel being the coordinator? E.g., overwhelmed, more in control, confident, scared?

- What parts of this coordinating role do you find overwhelming, and how might you find help? E.g., you could ask nurses and doctors, discuss with your wife, or set up your phone calendar, reminders and contacts.

- How will you ensure you can try to attend every appointment? Can you get a babysitter, or someone to fill in for you at work, or take leave from work?

5.3

Planning and Getting Organised

"In preparing for battle I have always found that plans are useless, but planning is indispensable."
- Dwight D. Eisenhower

There are many elements of this journey you cannot plan for. Just when you think you have everything under control, something unexpected will surely turn up. This will initially be scary until you get used to it and develop the strength to change and adapt on the fly. But not knowing what will happen is not an excuse for not having plans. Although nothing will ever go to plan, the process of planning is vital so you at least have something to go on and have thought through different scenarios.

The process of planning helped me gain control of an unpredictable situation. Having thought of a possible solution beforehand meant I wasn't floundering when the problem arose, even if that problem was a bit different to what I anticipated.

There are many ways you can plan, and many situations for which you can plan. Here are some of the situations you can plan for:

- The process for getting your wife to hospital;
- The people to call when your wife is having troubles;
- The procedure for administering medication;
- Planning which medications to give and when.

Some of the various planning methods you can use include flowcharts, checklists and calendars. Below are examples of how I planned for each of the above situations. You can adapt these plans yourself or come up with your own. You might even find you end up enjoying the process. I think of it like coming up with a battle plan as it's highly strategic and requires all situations to be considered.

RECORD-KEEPING

Good record-keeping makes your job as a champion carer far easier. You have a huge responsibility, not just in the direct care of your wife but in the other aspects of care such as being the doctors' liaison and source of truth. You need to make your life as easy as possible, and record-keeping helps with this.

Why Good Record-Keeping Is Necessary:

- One of your responsibilities as your wife's carer is to liaise with doctors on her behalf, which means being able to easily recall what medications and dosage she is on. This is especially the case when she is rushed to the emergency room or if she has no energy to talk to doctors herself;
- Your wife might be affected by "chemo-brain", which is when her memory becomes affected by the severely strong medication that is chemo. Her doctor will need to know details like how the pain levels have been, so having

records means you have those details even if your wife cannot remember them;

- Your wife's medication will often change, either the drugs themselves or the dosages. These can be difficult to keep track of, and good records will help with this;
- Finally, you'll be dealing with many doctors including emergency doctors, oncologists, general practitioners and surgeons, and they are not all talking to each other.

I must admit I was not Natasha's record-keeper. She was well organised and kept meticulous records. Your wife might be the same. I'm including this chapter so you can be aware of this necessary practice and it will help you both get organised.

Buy A Folder That Holds Documents Of All Sizes, And Has Dividers

Buy one that is bright in colour so it's easy to find and stands out when you're rushed. You'll need the folder to be easily accessible so that you can bring it to appointments and hospital. Make sure the folder is durable and high quality, because it will get thrown around a lot. Maybe you're at the hospital and need to help your wife out of the car but you have the folder in one hand. You'll drop the folder, help your wife and then pick up the folder. This poor folder will have a tough life so make sure it's up to the job! Use the sections to help you. For example, you can have the following sections including her medicine scripts, appointments, current medication she is on and information on side effects for the drugs or the surgery.

Download A Note-Taking App

For the times you don't have the folder around, or you want to take notes, doing so in your phone is great because it's usually always with you. You can try different ways of using notes to work out what is best for your situation, but some ideas include:

- Taking notes at doctor appointments;
- Taking notes on how your wife is feeling so you can inform doctors how she is coping with the medication;
- Keeping a note of the medications and dosages your wife is taking;
- Taking photos of documents you receive so you have a digital back-up;
- Keeping a note of how you're feeling.

KEEPING TRACK OF APPOINTMENTS

Use A Calendar App You Always Have Access To

Set up accounts so one calendar can show every single appointment you have, including your work schedule and that of your wife's work if she is working. This way you can book appointments easily by pulling up your calendar and looking ahead. Avoid clashes so you can be fully present at all her appointments without worrying about work schedules. You can clearly see your wife's appointment commitments when someone tries to schedule a work meeting with you. If you or your wife make an appointment, put it into your calendar immediately before you forget it. Let your phone do the hard work of remembering appointments. I use the default Apple Calendar on my iPhone because it easily synchronises across all my devices, can be shared with others, and shows my work and personal calendars together. Google Calendar does the same.

Use The Reminder Function In Your Phone

This is useful when booking an appointment a month in advance, or for remembering to do a blood test around a certain date. Whenever Natasha had a new medicine script, I would put in a reminder to see the doctor a week before that so we would have a new script ready to go as soon as that one ran out. Or if a doctor wanted to see us after a scan was done, I would put a reminder in the calendar following the scan appointment to then book the doctor's appointment. I would not book the doctor when I booked the scan, though, because chances are good that the scan will need to move if your wife is in pain that day. Cancelling one appointment is easier than cancelling two. If you've never used the reminder function on your phone, try searching online for a video tutorial. It's easy once you've used it a few times.

USING CHARTS TO MAKE RECORD-KEEPING EASY AND LOGICAL

Sometimes you will record a lot of data. Doctors will often ask when you administered medication to your wife, and what it was in response to. This is to help them work out whether the medication is working and how to adjust the dosages. This starts to get complex and difficult to remember so charts will help ease the burden. Like everything, experiment with different layouts and make them your own. You can download printable templates of all the following examples - as well as others - from www.soyourwifehascancer.com

Example: Pain Record Chart

As soon as Natasha was in pain and I gave her medicine, both the pain and the medicine could be recorded on the chart below. Then I could either bring the chart in with us to the next consultation or take a photo of it on my phone to show the doctor. Below is an example of Natasha's pain chart tailored to her condition (metastasis to the brain and bones at the point of making this).

Daily Pain, Medication and Bowel Movement Diary for Natasha Cruz-Gutteridge
Date: _____

Time	Location of Pain	Score (0 lowest)						Medication and Dose	Did it Work? (Y/N)	Bowels S,M,L	Bowels S (soft), M, L (hard)
	Shoulder	Back	Hip	Knee	Thigh	Ab	Head				
	Shoulder	Back	Hip	Knee	Thigh	Ab	Head				
	Shoulder	Back	Hip	Knee	Thigh	Ab	Head				
	Shoulder	Back	Hip	Knee	Thigh	Ab	Head				
	Shoulder	Back	Hip	Knee	Thigh	Ab	Head				
	Shoulder	Back	Hip	Knee	Thigh	Ab	Head				
	Shoulder	Back	Hip	Knee	Thigh	Ab	Head				
	Shoulder	Back	Hip	Knee	Thigh	Ab	Head				
	Shoulder	Back	Hip	Knee	Thigh	Ab	Head				

Example: Medication Tracker

I kept a spreadsheet to track how much of each medication Natasha had left so I knew when to phone her doctor and ask for a new script well before she ran out. I would check and update the chart every day after Natasha had taken her medication.

	15/11/2017		
	Tablets Left	Days Left	Reminder
Endone	130	43	36
Oxycontin 15mg	16	16	9
Oxycontin 20mg	25	25	18
Oxycontin 10mg	28	14	7
Pantoprazole		25	18
Dexamethasone 4mg	23	23	16
Methadone	33	33	26
Coloxyl Senna	37	9	6

Example: A Medication Chart

This is the exact medication chart I built for Natasha, which is available as an adaptable template online. Like the pain record chart, this one helps you plan ahead to know which medication to give, when, and the conditions that go with each drug (for example, whether it needs to be taken with food or not). I would have this on the wall in our bedroom next to Natasha's medications for easy reference.

TIME	DRUG	PURPOSE
AM	1. Endone 5mg - ~5am, no food necessary 2. Pantoprazole 40mg – upon waking, no food necessary 3. OxyContin 15mg – immediately after breakfast 4. Dexamethasone 2mg – immediately after breakfast 5. Memantine 1 tab – optional if felt like it	1. Prophylactic 2. Acid Reflux 3. Long-term pain relief 4. Long-term pain relief 5. Brain function
During the Day	1. Endone 5mg – as necessary, 1hr minimum gap 2. Panadol Rapid 2 tabs – as necessary, up to 4x per day 3. Lasix – 1-2 tabs – as necessary around 11am 4. Baclofen 1 tab – as necessary	1. Pain Flares 2. Pain Flares 3. Diuretic 4. Muscle Spasms

PM	1. OxyContin 15mg – immediately after dinner	1. Pain relief
	2. Dexamethasone 0.5 – 1mg – immediately after dinner	2. Pain relief
		3. Pain relief
	3. Methadone Half Tab – before bed	4. Anxiety and Insomnia
	4. Lorazepam half or quarter tab – as necessary	
		5. Brain function
	5. Memantine – optional if felt like it	6. Severe breakthrough pain
	6. Hydromorphone - injection	

You'll come up with your own ideas that work. As always, try something, see if it works, and then try something else. The goal is not perfection but rather to make the journey for both of you a little bit easier.

Flow Charts

These you can print out and put up next to your wife's chair or bed so that in the heat of the moment you don't have to search for the right information. They can be for anything you like, from the order of medication administered to steps to getting your wife ready for bed. Make it your own.

Example Flow Chart: Breakthrough Pain Plan - What To Do When Your Wife's Pain Is Getting Out Of Control

At two am in the morning, when your wife is in severe pain, the less thinking you need to do the better! Creating flow charts will help show you what needs to be done in response to certain conditions. This is so there is less to think about and a reduced risk of error. This is all part of your own planning and you can get it right from the start, whereas I was flying blind and had to make all these charts up myself.

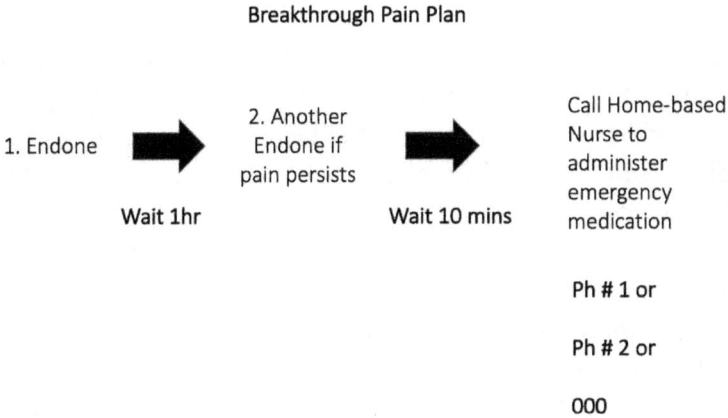

Breakthrough Pain Plan

1. Endone	➡	2. Another Endone if pain persists	➡	Call Home-based Nurse to administer emergency medication
	Wait 1hr		Wait 10 mins	

Ph # 1 or

Ph # 2 or

000

I made this example flow chart from the instructions that were given to us by Natasha's nurses. The key information I needed to know was the waiting period between administering pain relief. It was sometimes difficult to remember if we needed to wait one hour or ten minutes for the first Endone, but this chart reduced the cognitive load. I would give Natasha the first Endone, then set a timer on my phone. Hopefully she didn't need the second one, but if she did that's when it got serious and there was only a ten-minute wait after the second dose to see if she responded. I have taken out the nurses' phone numbers for this example but I had them listed on the chart for ease of reference, though I had the numbers stored in my phone contacts too.

CHECKLISTS

It's too easy to forget something, and a checklist is such an easy solution that it would be silly not to use one. You have a lot to remember and run through, and checklists help to reduce the cognitive load of thinking every time about what to bring or do.

Despite airline pilots flying the exact same plane every single day, for multiple trips per day, they will always follow their checklists. Pilots use checklists for every procedure including when entering the cockpit, before powering the plane up, before taxi, before take-off, and after take-off.

Checklists can be used for anything. I even have one for going to the gym because the one time I think I have everything I will get to the gym and forget something like my headphones. I will be punished by having to listen to blaring music instead of my audiobook!

Example: A Checklist To Run Through Before You Go To The Hospital
Print yours out and put it near your front door.

Medical
- o Records folder
- o Copy or photo of medication chart
- o Copy or photo of pain chart
- o Notepad and pen to take notes
- o Hand sanitiser
- o Face mask

Comfort
- o Water bottles
- o Phone and charger (you might be there a while)

o Pillow for the car
o Book for your wife to read when waiting for the doctor
o Book for you to read
o Card game to play while waiting for the doctor
o Healthy snacks

Wallet
o Credit card
o Medicare Card (or equivalent in your country)
o Health insurance card

MEDICAL EQUIPMENT AT HOME

Just like an adventurer takes tools to help them, you must also acquire tools for your journey as well. As Ernest Shackleton, the Antarctic explorer, stated; "Our spoons are one of our indispensable possessions here. To lose one's spoon would be almost as serious as it is for an edentate person to lose his set of false teeth." You will build many of the tools yourself, like medical records and plans. But some you'll need to purchase if you can and there will be expensive options as well as cheap or free ones. You'll never need the most expensive ones but try not to buy the cheapest ones either because you need reliability. This is your wife's health we are talking about. Below are three pieces of advice for working out the equipment you might need at home.

Ask Your Wife's Doctor And A Physiotherapist What Equipment They Recommend Your Wife To Have At Home

Your wife will need different equipment at different stages of her journey, and her doctors can advise you on this if you ask them. If you see a physiotherapist for mobility issues, they will give recommendations to help your wife at home, like a walking frame if the cancer is in her bones. Ask for help. There is no point trying to guess and work everything out the hard way when the experts have been through this with hundreds of patients.

Ask A Pharmacist Which Brand Of Equipment Is The Best Value For Money

As in the section on building relationships with doctors and nurses, I recommend building a good working relationship with your pharmacist as you'll always be there buying medications. They sell most equipment you will need. A good pharmacist will give you a recommendation for the best option rather than the most expensive one. If they point you to the most expensive options, ask what specifically makes these better. For example, high-end blood pressure readers have memory options so multiple people can use them and they track the trends for each user. This feature is useless as it's probably only your wife using the blood pressure reader and recording the read-out in your phone or on a chart is quite easy.

Look At Second-Hand Options And Ask Hospitals For Loan Schemes

Some of the equipment will be expensive which can be a problem especially if you're on a budget or if you cannot work as much as you used to. There is no need to be embarrassed about this. You'll probably be amazed at what schemes are out there, but you often have to ask in order to learn about them. If there is no free help, have a look at second-hand options depending on what you need. Obviously you don't want a second-hand thermometer but a used wheelchair will be fine.

Common tools useful for most cancer patients, that are not too expensive, include:

- A box for all medication, with dividers. They can all be in one place and easy to reach;
- Paracetamol for quick pain relief, if she is not allergic;
- Thermometer to quickly check if your wife has a fever when she feels unwell;
- Face masks, which can reduce the chance of your wife contracting germs when out and about. This is necessary if her immune system is compromised by chemotherapy.

Some Other Equipment You Might Need To Buy, Which We Bought For Natasha, Include:

- Blood pressure monitor;
- An emergency caller device to wear. Natasha wore this around her neck. She could press one button and her caller device would call me immediately if she had a fall. This gave her the freedom to have time alone and to go around the house without someone holding her hand. I had the peace of mind that she could easily contact me even if her phone went flat or was out of reach. These days you can get wrist bands like the TCL Movetime Family Watch that have sim cards and emergency location options;
- An air purifier, especially when there was pollen in the air. Natasha's lungs were weak enough without having a cough hurting them further. I would regularly swap the cabin air filter in our car. Ideally look for HEPA filters, or those with the highest level of filtration.
- Non-slip mats for the showers. This was especially important for Natasha when the cancer spread to her bones and made a fall more likely and dangerous;
- In the last six months of Natasha's life we were blessed to have the following all loaned to us by the Australian Capital Territory Health System:
  - A walking frame;

- o A wheelchair;
- o An electronic recliner chair to relieve pressure on her hips;
- o A hospital bed for the home with a hoist;
- o A cushion for the car and her wheelchair that added comfort without the risk of sores.

As with all the advice in this book, it's about making your life easier in a situation that is far from easy. Just as going to the Antarctic would be impossible without suitable clothes, ice picks and flares, this journey will be harder without the correct equipment to help.

YOUR WIFE'S DIET

This is the final part of caring for your wife at home. The most accurate and specific advice will come from her doctor although some general advice is covered below.

Many people will be free flowing with their advice for what your wife should eat. They'll tell you about how certain foods cause cancer and that she needs to go on certain diets.

If ever you're unsure about anyone's recommendation, ask your wife's oncologist about it. Natasha's oncologist focused more on her well-being and gave her the okay to eat whatever she wanted, in moderation. If she wanted a cheeseburger in the middle of the night, I can assure you I would go out and get it!

My main concern was keeping her calorie intake up because chemotherapy is so draining and I was worried there was not a lot of food she felt like eating. I figured that simple pleasures would be okay, especially when she didn't have much energy to do everything else she used to enjoy.

Eating Out

One of the few activities your wife may have the energy to do is to go out for dinner occasionally. You both need to eat anyway! Sometimes it might be difficult to do so - given your wife's changing tastes, tolerances and energy - but with some planning ahead on your part you can make eating out work. Most importantly, it's a chance for both of you to have great night and feel 'normal' doing 'normal' things.

Natasha and I loved to eat out together as it did make our life a bit more normal and gave us some time alone as a couple, given we were living with her parents. If we were going to a new restaurant I would call ahead to ask if they had items on their menu I knew she could stomach while on chemo and, if they didn't, whether they were willing to alter the menu. Some restaurants couldn't change their dishes, but many would, especially when the circumstances were explained. If we wanted to go to a fancier place, I would call to let them know our table would require priority service given Natasha's low energy levels.

There was one night where Natasha wanted to take her parents out for dinner for their wedding anniversary, so I went to the restaurant the day before and explained everything: that we would need room for her wheelchair and for starters to be ready as soon as we got there. Everything went to plan and the restaurant was super helpful. Natasha felt overjoyed that she could still stick to her plans, which made the planning and hard work worthwhile.

To conclude Part 5, there are many moving parts to caring for your wife: understanding the different treatments, working with her doctors, and setting up your home and routines to be comfortable for her. Treat this like a learning exercise. You don't have to get everything right from day one, and it's always okay to make mistakes. Try to enjoy the process of coming up with strategies and implementing them because this is one of the few parts of the journey you actually can control. Plans and planning tools are there to help you on your journey. Think of them like battle plans or maps for the journey.

Despite so much outside your control, you *are* in control when making these plans. Even if reality changes from the plan, it's the process of planning that counts. Planning gets you in the headspace of knowing that you can work this out, even when everything is crazy.

KEY POINTS FROM PART 5

- With any treatment your wife does - whether it's surgery, chemotherapy, radiation or immunotherapy - take the time to understand what is going on. Ask questions of doctors and do your own research. The best research is done with your wife's oncologist and websites like eviQ, Cancer Council and Cancer Research UK rather than blogs and forums.

- Be adaptable when treatment is happening as the side effects are unpredictable and there will be many appointments and trips to the hospital.

- Do your best to attend every appointment and hospital visit, if you can. There are strategies you can use to schedule around your work with ease.

- Choosing great doctors is vital as you'll be spending a lot of time with them and you'll need to trust them.

- Treating all doctors and hospital staff well is an easy but powerful strategy for making the journey more pleasant for you, your wife and everyone involved in her care.

- Your job of coordinating all the doctors is a demanding one, but there are many tools and techniques at your disposal to make this easier.

- Make your home-caring life more straightforward with good records, charts and checklists as well as appropriate medical equipment.

PART SIX

CARING FOR EACH OTHER

"Happy is the man who finds a true friend, and far happier
is he who finds that true friend in his wife."
- Franz Schubert

Communication With Your Wife

"If others tell us something, we make assumptions, and if they don't tell us something, we make assumptions…We make all sorts of assumptions because we don't have the courage to ask questions."
- Miguel Ruiz, The Four Agreements

When on the Hero's Journey, you are never on your own - no matter how much you might feel that way. You have your supporters, this book, doctors, and you have your wife. This part gives specific advice on how to travel on the journey together with your wife. I cover topics such as how to communicate in these unusual circumstances, how to cope with each other's emotions, how to still be intimate in different ways, how to communicate with your children, and dealing with the rest of the family.

THE RELATIONSHIP CHECK-IN

Do you a have structured way of communicating with your wife? Chances are, probably not. A relationship check-in is as important as any other aspect of caring for your wife.

Before I learned the importance of the relationship check-in, I was guessing everything and flying blind. Was Natasha happy with my caring? Was she upset about that mistake I made? What did she need me to do more of? Less of? Did she know how I was feeling? How was she going? We only started doing this four years into our marriage and we both wish we had learned about it earlier. It was much easier to answer these questions outright rather than making assumptions the whole time.

This method I discuss here is called the weekly relationship check-in. You probably haven't communicated with your wife in this way before. Natasha and I hadn't before we learned about it. The check-in was introduced to Natasha and me by our marriage counsellor (which I'll tell you more about shortly) who told us that divorce mostly happens not because of one big event but due to the build-up of many small gripes. People are excellent at holding onto grudges, which explains the countless jokes about how in an argument everything someone did wrong in the past is brought to the forefront.

In marriage it's easy to assume answers to those questions, but why not make life a bit easier if you can? After I started talking openly with Natasha, our journey was transformed. Suddenly I knew exactly how she was feeling and I realised that many of my previous assumptions were plain wrong. The golden rule is if you don't talk about something, you cannot expect the other person to read your mind or to change their behaviours.

How To Do A Relationship Check-In

The weekly relationship check-in is simple but powerful and solves these problems. I will break it down in separate points below but in short, it's a four-step process that takes no longer than an hour and is often much quicker:

- Start by taking turns with what you've been grateful for - about each other - over the last week;
- Then take turns to discuss what has upset you, either that they have done, or what you're upset about in the relationship in general;
- Then take turns to share what you're each anxious about generally and in the relationship for the coming next week;
- Finally, plan something nice for the upcoming week.

- *Step 1 - Discuss What You Are Each Grateful For*

This first discussion on gratitude is the best part and, over time, there will be little upsetting you and much to be grateful for. You'll start to look forward to the check-in as it is a chance to be thanked for how amazing you have been and it is a time to thank your wife.

When was the last time you told your wife what you were grateful for? Expressing gratitude rarely happens in a marriage. Partners start taking each other for granted and feel underappreciated. Then they start to do less for each other, thinking it won't make a difference anyway. Expressing gratitude is a form of positive reinforcement, which is when we get a reward for doing something, so when you find out what she appreciates, which will often surprise you, you'll then want to do more of that.

You might be grateful for something small, like when she thanked you for making her a cup of tea, or something big, like when she asked the doctor about how to make sure you were okay. Maybe she was feeling energetic one day and did something helpful for you. This might seem small, or would have been normal when she was healthy, but it could be a big deal for her now. Your gratitude for her actions, even if they seem small, will make her happy.

You could start the check-in by telling your wife how grateful you are that she has agreed to spend this time together for the check-in because it's helping you become a champion carer and husband for her.

- *Step 2 – Discuss What You Need More Of From Each Other Or What Is Upsetting You*

Most people are scared about doing a relationship check-in because of the step where you each share what's upsetting you. This might include what you are angry about with her but also angry about with the relationship in general, such as not having enough time together because of the hospital visits. I agree this can be confrontational but this step is only one part of the check-in.

Some topics that could be discussed in this time include sex, which is covered more in chapter 6.3, the amount of time you're spending or not spending together, activities you want to do more of together, and how each of you are feeling about the cancer.

When Natasha and I first started these check-ins, there were some big-ticket items that needed discussing, which were quite difficult to hear. Natasha wanted me to ask her doctors more questions during the consults because she thought I wasn't interested in what was going on. She wanted me to pray with her every night, rather than us praying individually, and to be more open with her with my struggles. Once she knew what was bothering me she could help fix it, which not only helped me but made her feel empowered and useful.

Likewise, once I knew what was bothering her I could try to fix it too. I had assumed Natasha wouldn't want me asking the doctors too many questions because her questions were more important but I quickly found out that I was wrong to assume. The items discussed quickly moved into the section of the check-in on expressing gratitude after I started making the changes she wanted. Eventually there wasn't much that was upsetting us, and sometimes nothing at all, because we had discussed these enough and were on the same page.

- *Step 3 - Discuss Your Anxieties For The Next Week*

You might be anxious about an upcoming scan result or she might be anxious about her or your parents coming to visit. Whatever it is, discuss the anxiety openly so you both can come up with strategies to alleviate those anxieties. Even without solutions, you're now both aware of how each other is feeling. Something you thought would not be a big deal might in fact be huge to her.

- *Step 4 – Plan Something Nice For The Week Ahead*

This is where you end the check-in on a high, just like how you began with gratitude. This is a chance to tell each other what you would like to do together. You could take it in turns to come up with an idea each week.

How To Respond To Each Other's Points

It's vital that during this time you let each other speak safely, rather than reacting to everything the other person says. One way is to allow each other to go through their whole list before responding. The best response is to thank each other for feeling comfortable enough to raise the issues (which might take a couple of check-ins to develop that comfort), that you've taken note of them, and will do better this week. You can apologise for anything you did wrong and tell her it's just that you didn't know you were upsetting her.

You could ask her questions to find out what you could change to make her happy. Again, you don't want to be guessing about what needs to come next when all you have to do is ask.

Try not to get defensive or argue with her and say she is wrong to be upset about this particular issue. If she's upset about something, it doesn't matter if you don't agree with her complaint. All that matters is fixing it in the future even if you had the best of intentions at the time. You can explain where you were coming from and that you had good intentions, but focus more on how she feels. The easiest way of thinking about a response is to imagine what you want her to say to you in response if you told her what was annoying you.

Raising The Idea With Your Wife

This is where many men get stuck: they love the idea but don't know how to suggest it to their wife. She might think this is a "we need to talk" conversation, or tell you that nothing is wrong anyway so why bother?

It's important when you bring this up with your wife to tell her that the weekly check-in is not only to air grievances and launch accusations but it's a relationship-building exercise to help you become closer rather than holding onto grudges.

You could approach the check-in by asking her to read this chapter herself, or you could frame it as part of your quest to make sure you're doing the absolute best you can for her as a husband and carer. Another tactic is to ask her to try the check-in for a couple of weeks. No commitment, just an experiment.

Setting Aside Regular Time

An hour each week is a good amount of time to have the check-in but if you only have time for five minutes that's much better than nothing at all. Work out the best time for both of you and set a recurring event in your calendar. Then, unless there is a medical appointment, ensure nothing gets in the way of this time. Knowing you have the time set aside means you don't have to raise issues during the week every time they come up. Instead you can set them aside as you know you have a dedicated time to raise them. You know this is a safe time where you can raise everything, no matter how hard some things can be to discuss.

You'll have time to think about what you want to discuss. You can save up all that you are grateful for and, if anything bad happens during the week, by the time you get to the check-in you might realise it's not actually that big a deal or you've worked out a solution you can bring to her. When you do have a chance to go on a date - like dinner or a movie - alone together, you won't need to use that time to talk about issues. You can focus on having fun because you know there is a separate relationship check-in scheduled.

Where You Could Have Your Relationship Check-In
It's important to separate the check-in from daily life, almost like you're going away to do an analysis from an outsider perspective and then coming back into your life having made improvements. Good enough is better than aiming for perfection and not doing it at all, so if you only have time to do it at home, go for it.

Doing a check-in at a crowded place like a restaurant can make it difficult to discuss certain topics in the depth they need to be discussed. Also, you want to separate this from being a date. I recommend getting takeaway or packing some food from home and finding somewhere private. Going for a walk together can work too.

How The Check-In Helped Us

Once we started our weekly check-ins, I realised Natasha was as upset as I was about the loss of our boundaries due to living with her parents, and she too felt like we needed more time together as a couple. We were able to work this out together, which led to the drives we spent alone, as I shared with you in chapter 2.4 on flexibility.

Natasha was better able to understand I was not coping too well, which was something she was not entirely aware of. That led to her being more understanding and pushing me to spend more time with my mates and doing things for myself occasionally. Our marriage and my caring transformed, and we both wished we had implemented regular discussion at the start of our marriage - even before she got sick.

EXERCISE: PREPARING FOR YOUR RELATIONSHIP CHECK-IN

How will you raise the idea of doing a weekly check-in with your wife? Think of all the benefits that are unique and important to you and plan out a script for how you'll ask her.

When is a good time for you to do it? Assume your wife will agree to doing it, in which case you can already schedule in the time. Plan out how you'll ask for her preference whether you do it straight after you raise it with her, or if she wants time to prepare for it. Come up with some options for the schedule. She will appreciate you taking control.

Plan out your first check-in. Where will you do it? What are you grateful for? What complaints do you have? What are you anxious about? What's a nice date idea? Write down the schedule for the check-in and bring it. She will appreciate your preparedness and initiative.

Give a fist bump to yourself for stepping up and doing what is difficult but necessary to strengthen your marriage and caring ability.

SEEK MARRIAGE COUNSELLING IF YOU NEED EXTRA HELP TO COMMUNICATE

Marriage counselling is about maintaining and strengthening a marriage. Marriage is one of the most difficult endeavours people can engage in, even when not afflicted by cancer. It would be sensible, then, to seek help to make marriage a bit easier.

Natasha and I sought marriage counselling after my personal psychologist advised me to, when I told her I was finding it difficult to open up to Natasha. Thankfully, Natasha was open to the idea.

You might automatically assume marriage counselling is only for relationships falling apart and near divorce, but marriage counselling - just like any counselling - is not only for when the situation has hit rock-bottom.

Just like a psychologist will help you on your own, a marriage counsellor (who is a trained psychologist) can help you both build a great marriage. An objective, trained professional can sense things neither of you are able to because they see many married couples and they can give you a third-party perspective. They have years of training in understanding the scientific research behind successful relationships. The advice our marriage counsellor gave us was invaluable and because we both heard the same advice Natasha and I were on the same page and were able to discuss that advice together.

Counselling can be expensive though. Marriage counsellors, like psychologists, have an hourly rate but you can negotiate with them. Receptionists at clinics with multiple therapists can tell you which ones reduce their fees. Under the circumstances of a spouse with cancer, a marriage counsellor might be willing to reduce their fee for a set period. If you or your wife are on a mental health-care plan in Australia you could use this to get a rebate on the marriage counselling - just ask the receptionists when you book. Another option is to see the hospital social worker as a couple, if available. Part of their job is to help couples navigate the impact of cancer on their relationship.

Another barrier to counselling is that it will require your wife spending energy she might not have to get out of the house, unless you can do the session online. If you find the energy and financial cost prohibitive, focus on implementing the weekly check-in, which on its own puts you well ahead of almost every married couple.

UNDERSTAND THE FIVE LOVE LANGUAGES

Think of how hard it is to communicate with someone who speaks a different language. This is the same when you speak different love languages. You are trying to show each other your love but in a language that you don't use. There are five different love languages:

- *Words Of Affirmation* – where your wife tells you she is proud of you or you send her messages saying you love her;
- *Acts Of Service* – where you do things for your wife that help her or she gives you a head massage. Caring for your wife is an example of this;
- *Receiving Gifts* – if someone speaks this language, they appreciate it when someone gives them gifts;
- *Quality Time* – some people simply want to spend time

together, even if they are not talking. An example might be going on a hike or reading a book together;

* *Physical Touch* – a hug or a kiss is what is needed if people speak this love language.

Do The Love Language Questionnaire And Then Talk About It
What is your love language? I like quality time even if I'm not talking with my wife but just reading a book together. I also like words of affirmation and acts of service. You probably know intuitively what your love language or languages are as well as your wife's. Still, it's worth doing the quick 30-question questionnaire at www.5lovelanguages.com/quizzes. You could even make this one of your first tasks for the weekly check-in you now have, and this could be part of the discussion for the second half of that time. On your own, you could then come up with all the ways you can express love to your wife in her love language.

Hopefully, you can already see you're making heroic changes to your marriage and helping to strengthen it. You're doing what most other husbands are not able or willing to do. Always remember this mission when making tough calls like asking your wife for a weekly check-in or seeking counselling.

What To Do If Your Wife Gets Angry At You

"There is a huge amount of freedom that comes to you when you take nothing personally."
- Miguel Ruiz, The Four Agreements

Going on this journey together with your wife will bring many beautiful moments of bonding. But the journey will almost certainly cause plenty of angst. Your wife will probably be more emotional during her cancer journey and sometimes her anger can be directed at you, rightly or wrongly. Knowing what to do or how to react in this situation is crucial.

Don't Fight Back
It will be a shock when your wife gets angry with you, especially if she doesn't normally get angry or if she has a higher level of anger than normal, and it can be normal to react to this. For example, if she said you're being distant and unavailable to her, you could easily list off every time she has been the same. Will this help? It would likely make the situation worse. As with anything in this

journey, the easy option is almost never the right one to take. You'll need practice to get better at this. There will be times you react and get angry with her too, but don't be hard on yourself if this happens. There will be plenty of opportunities to practise a better reaction. Don't try to fix whatever it is. Just listen and be there for her. She will probably regret getting angry at you when she calms down in an hour or day or so.

Don't Take It Personally

What should you do instead of reacting? You almost certainly cannot fix whatever made her upset. Men want to solve problems and, if your wife is angry, you will want to know what caused it and then solve it. This is difficult though, because there probably isn't an actual problem to solve. Chances are your wife has a solution herself already.

Often what people want is to have their feelings acknowledged, to be heard and comforted. Her anger could have been caused by many things: she was overly tired, emotional, sick of being in hospital, resentful of having cancer, anxious about the next scan, anxious about her friends coming to see her, or any one of a million causes. You just happened to bear the brunt of this in the moment.

Be easy on yourself. Yes, you may have accidentally triggered her anger by adjusting her body in a painful way or saying something wrong but it wasn't this that was the sole cause of her anger. What you said or did was just a trigger that maybe caused your wife to feel out of control. As long as you did your best in the moment, then that is enough. You might have stuffed up, but maybe you were tired too or sick of the whole situation and weren't thinking straight. It's okay. There is no reason to take her anger personally because you were doing your best and could not have done any better given your circumstances.

I would always take things personally and my first reaction was to beat myself up for making Natasha upset. Sometimes it seemed like nothing I could do was right. I would blame myself for not moving her correctly, for being too tired to hear she needed my help, or for forgetting to bring something warm for her when it was cold. Eventually I learned to be easy on myself and recognise that these were minor things compared to everything else I was doing right. I came to realise that Natasha's anger wasn't really about those small things but more about just being angry about the whole situation and the fact she needed to rely so heavily on someone else. Once I took the burden off myself, I knew that as long as I kept doing my best, I was okay. If I made a mistake I would apologise and tell her I would try to do better next time.

Put Yourself In Her Shoes

Your wife has a disease that's doing its best to kill her. It has radically changed her life and yours. My therapist told me once that depression can sometimes manifest as anger rather than sadness. It's only natural your wife would be feeling depressed or anxious with the situation she is in. Even as Natasha's husband and seeing every day what it was like for her, I still cannot imagine what it's actually like to have cancer myself and nor do I want to imagine this.

Forgive And Send Her Love

Forgive your wife for getting angry at you, as hard as this can be in the moment. The easiest way to forgive someone is to remind yourself of all the times you've made the same error. You come to realise you're not a saint either because none of us are. Forgiveness is always about releasing the burden of holding onto anger from yourself, so treat it as a gift rather than giving in or letting something slide.

Even harder than forgiveness, but surprisingly powerful, is to send your wife love. At first this seems like a stupid idea, especially because love is the opposite of what you're feeling in the moment but try using it before judging. The steps are as follows:

1. Close your eyes and feel your heart expand to capture all the love around you, from everyone you know. Concentrate all of this love inside your heart.
2. Send all of this pent-up love from your heart to your wife, every last bit.
3. Visualise this love entering your wife, and *feel* it entering her. Then, relax and feel all that energy you gave her coming back to you.

Do this quickly and do it every time something happens that makes you feel someone has done something wrong to you. You might have to follow the steps multiple times to dissolve the anger but keep persevering.

Notice How Her Anger Makes You Feel

A skill is to notice how her anger makes you feel. Men are generally not great at this. I took a long time to learn how to do this with my psychologist because I always wanted to think through an issue rather than feel it. You will justifiably be angry when your wife gets angry with you, so allow yourself to feel this.

Feeling anger is different to getting angry with her. Notice the anger inside of you; the pressure building up, the desire to yell, or walk away, or hit something. The anger is normal and you're human. You might also feel sad. You've put so much effort into caring for your wife only to get treated like this. Or sad because you can see how upset she is with her situation that has made her react differently to normal, like getting angry with you. You might feel a range of emotions. Just notice them. Go for a walk and sit with them for a while. Or write them down on your phone or in a journal. You can also try the advice given in chapter 4.3 where we discussed anger.

You could use your weekly check-in time to tell your wife that her getting angry at you made you upset, you were only doing your best and didn't mean to do anything wrong. This gives her a chance to see how her emotions affect yours and to apologise, away from the heat of the moment. She'll probably regret getting angry with you and apologise in the moment or when she has calmed down, but the check-in gives you a chance to talk about what happened in a safe space.

As with everything in this book, be open to learning and practising. Go easy on your wife and go easy on yourself.

EXERCISE: DEALING WITH YOUR WIFE'S ANGER

Think back to a time when your wife got angry with you. Could there have been a justification for it, such as her anxiety about the cancer? Did you take it personally? Could you have reacted differently?

What will be your strategy if your wife gets angry with you in the future?

Most of the time anger is to do with repressed feelings that have been triggered accidentally:

- Recognise the underlying feeling, e.g., scared, sad, bad, mad
- Who is doing the talking? Is it your wife's normal voice or is it her inner child or her scared person?
- What is that voice really saying?
- What would a good parent say to that person expressing the repressed feelings?
- Acknowledge the underlying feeling and how it is coming out, e.g. I hear you are angry.
- Investigate what is coming up and ask her what is making you feel that emotion.
- Ask your wife what she needs. It might be encouragement or just a hug.

Remind yourself of your strategy for dealing with your own feelings of anger.

6.3

Changes to Your Sex Life

Nobody talked to me about how a couple's sex life can be affected by cancer, probably because sex is highly personal and therefore a difficult topic to discuss. Your relationship has changed since the diagnosis and sex is yet another aspect of your lives that needs to be adapted to the cancer. In this chapter I look at how cancer affects your sex life, sex drive, and some alternative solutions to try.

Contraception

Depending on your stage of life, you may now need to rethink the contraception you've been using. Sadly, a pregnancy during chemotherapy would probably need to be aborted due to poisoning the foetus and causing defects. Taking the contraceptive pill may not be suitable for your wife with her treatment protocol. You may need to use condoms or other fail-safe methods. Your wife may have been taking care of the family planning, but this might now be something that needs more discussion. This can be another topic for your weekly relationship check-in.

The news that we could no longer try for children was difficult to hear. Natasha and I were a young couple planning for children at the time of the diagnosis, but we had to limit ourselves to focusing on one thing at a time.

You Might Have A Lower Sex Drive
Once on this cancer journey, there are many aspects that will affect your and your wife's sex drive. Yours and her sleep will possibly be interrupted, reducing your energy. Chemotherapy is a drain on energy and can wreak havoc with hormones which can impact a woman's sex drive.

An often-unspoken aspect of this is that you suddenly have to deal with so much uncertainty and challenge in your life, that the idea of sex might not be that interesting anymore.

And let's be honest here: another challenge is that your wife will physically look different due to treatment. She may have lost her hair, and either put on weight or lost weight. This can make it difficult for her to feel attractive, and for you to be turned on by her like you used to be. The research is clear that this is a common problem for partner carers.

How To Deal With This - Talk About It Together

As discussed in chapter 6.1 on communicating with your wife, there is no point guessing what each other is feeling when you can talk about it. You may assume she doesn't want to have sex whereas in fact she actually might. Talking about sex might be unusual for you as a couple but you can bring it up during your weekly check-in after you've become more comfortable raising difficult issues. If you're finding the topic too difficult to discuss you could find a marriage counsellor to help you.

Try Other Methods Of Intimacy

One change that can be made is to try other methods of intimacy, which could include spending time together or cuddling while watching a TV show. Being close to each other and having that contact will often suffice to show each other that you are loved. Try massaging her, which has the added benefit of helping your wife with any pain. You could let your wife give you a light head rub or shoulder massage. This she could do without much effort and she can feel useful if sometimes she feels like you're the only one doing all the caring.

Try new ways of turning each other on. Have you been putting in as much effort to how you present yourselves to each other, or are you overly comfortable after years of marriage? Try to remember when you first met and how you would do your hair and dress nicely. You could talk about how you can try seducing each other in creative ways. If your wife has lost her hair, a wig could help her feel beautiful again. If you're unhappy with your wife's appearance now, try to visualise how beautiful she looked when you were first together and know that she is still that person. Your wife inside is the same person you fell in love with, and you can always come back to that attraction. You married every part of her, not just her looks.

If both of you still want to make love, but are struggling with energy levels, there are other methods of giving pleasure to each other or yourselves. You could try extended foreplay perhaps. You'll need to talk about what works and try something new, which can be confronting at first but you might find this is a whole new aspect of your relationship opening up.

All Couples Face This Problem, Not Only Those With Cancer
Many of my mates would open up to me about their wife's lack of desire for sex after having children due to always being tired, or because they're working too hard, or they have become too familiar with each other after a long time together. This is normal, and there's no need to blame the cancer or your wife. If you follow the above advice you should maintain some aspects of your relationship that were familiar.

EXERCISE: YOUR SEX LIFE

What are you missing in your sex life? Has anything changed? If you weren't having much sex before, could you use this as an opportunity to change that?

How will you raise it in your next weekly relationship check-in? How can you find out what she is feeling about this part of your relationship? How can you tell her how you are feeling?

Who can you talk to about this, if you feel that this is difficult? Could you raise it with your therapist if you have one? Could you see a marriage counsellor? How about asking for advice from family and friends who you normally wouldn't talk to about this?

6.4

Children

*"The most important thing a father can do for
his children is to love their mother."*
- Theodore Hesburgh

In this chapter I give you some ideas about what to do and say if you have children and if you don't. There are positives and negatives to both circumstances and, like everything, this will require constant experimentation to get it right for your family.

If You Have Young Children

There isn't much scientific research out there on how children cope when a parent is sick, but the evidence that does exist tells us that children and adolescents actually cope quite well and even better than parents typically expect in a situation like this. They don't usually experience higher levels of serious psychological and social difficulties compared with other children. What they are at risk of, however, is internalising their issues rather than expressing them openly, though researchers are unclear why this is.

Of all the age and gender groups, adolescent daughters seem to be the most affected by a parent's cancer. As always, your family is different to other families so you'll know best what works and doesn't work in your own situation. This is a new situation for all of you so be prepared to give your best and to make mistakes. I have gone into detail about the mindset needed to grow and to be comfortable with failure, and this will be a good time to use that.

Talk With Your Wife About What You Both Want

As discussed in chapter 6.1 on communicating with your wife, you could use your weekly relationship check-in to discuss what is and isn't working with your children. There's no point in guessing what your wife wants from her children and from you when you can ask her. You can ask her when she wants her children around, and when she wants some alone time. You can ask about different scenarios, like does she want the children to see her when in excruciating pain? Most importantly, ask her what to say to the children when they ask certain questions. Maybe she wants to explain the situation to them herself, or maybe she wants you to, or maybe she wants to hide the truth. You can mention your own opinions about this and your wife might find it helpful if you've thought through this beforehand too. This discussion is crucial.

Your Children Can Help Take Care Of Their Mother

You could be surprised at how quickly your children learn new tricks and understand complex medical terms. You can show them what their mother needs, and they can help prepare simple things like filling hot water bottles or refilling water jugs, depending on their age. They will love feeling useful and can help to reduce your burden.

Try Your Best To Maintain A Sense Of Routine For Them

It will sometimes be impossible to maintain any semblance of routine. There will be times when your children are late for school or miss an after-school activity. If you can, try to keep to a routine so they don't feel isolated from their friends or resentful of the situation. If the routine does need to change, take the time to explain to them why, and ask for their understanding. They mightn't understand things in the way an adult understands, but this is okay. You'll find out what works and you know your children best.

Ask For Help From Friends And Family

If you have friends who have children, they will understand how hard having children is! They'll be more open to helping than you realise, but you have to ask. Perhaps they can pick your children up from school along with their children, and either bring them home or let them play together at their home. Perhaps they can take them with their families on the weekend. You will never know what they are willing to do unless you ask them. If your children's grandparents are still around, or if extended family live nearby, ask them to help out too.

Be Brave Enough To Show Your Emotions In Front Of Your Children

They know you're human and they can actually comfort you when you're struggling. There is no such thing as the tough man who never cries, and this is an important lesson for them - that even their tough dad can experience overwhelming emotion.

Ask Doctors About How To Help Explain What Is Happening

Doctors see families and couples in your situation all the time and have been trained to help with explanations. You can ask them what you can say to children. Bring up the questions your children are asking and ask what the doctor recommends. This will be useful because your wife will be going through her own unique phases and your family will be different to other families but at least your wife's doctor will know your individual situation intimately.

Talk To Your Children About How They Are Coping

To talk to your children, you can set aside time weekly or chat with them as you tuck them into bed. Ultimately, you want them to know you care about how they are feeling and coping, and about their questions and uncertainty. You want them to be comfortable opening up to you, especially if their mother's health deteriorates further. Ask them 'How is school going?', 'What are you telling your friends?' or 'What questions do you have?'. They might be silent at first, because they are still working out how to voice what they want to say, but eventually they will open up. You can ask them to write or draw if talking about their feelings is difficult. Above all, let them know you'll always be there for them, even if sometimes their mother is not feeling well enough to see them.

Make sure you're in regular contact with their teachers if they are school-aged and ask their teachers to let you know if they observe any changes in behaviour. Teachers, principals and school counsellors are trained to help parents in difficult situations like this.

Finally, If You Do Make A Mistake, Apologise And Keep Trying Your Best

It will of course be tough to deal with your children retreating from you or getting upset with you if you make a mistake. But you started this journey knowing you would make hundreds of mistakes. You cannot possibly know what to do in every scenario beforehand, so be gentle on yourself. You'll be more tired than usual and sometimes that will mean you have a shorter temper. If this happens, apologise and explain to your children how hard this is for you. They will hopefully be more understanding if you lose your temper again. Tell them you're doing your best and you know you won't always get it right, which is something you're now used to telling yourself.

6.5

The Rest Of
The Family

This chapter is about the extended family; your own and your wife's. Cancer affects everybody connected to a patient. You have a unique role in coordinating everyone. You'll sometimes feel a bit smothered or left out, especially if your wife's parents are around, so set boundaries early on. Your primary purpose as a champion caregiver is to keep your wife comfortable and to care for yourself so you can care for her. In this chapter, I show you how you can do all of this.

Getting help from your families
You could try doing everything on your own or as a couple during this journey, especially because you're a couple and are used to going through life without much help. In Western countries the focus is on the individual family unit, so the reaction of trying to do everything without help is normal. This situation is different to ordinary life, though, and you'll need all the help you can get.

We ended up moving in with Natasha's parents, which was hard to adapt to, but because her dad was retired he could sit with Natasha during the day, giving me the freedom to still work. I don't suggest you go this far but inviting family to move closer to you or moving closer to them could be an idea to explore. You could always try one option and if that doesn't work as expected, you can try something else. It's a similar situation to wanting to have grandparents around when having a child so you can have extra support.

Different Ways Of Coping

One of the difficulties with extended family is that not everyone copes the same way. You might not understand their strategies, and they might not understand yours, but do what works for you without fear of judgement. You might sense other family members are not emotional at all, whereas in fact they are not processing the situation well. Everyone is different, but always discuss this with your wife. She understands her parents and will have great insight on your parents and family too. If ever in doubt, discuss it.

Potential Family Issues With Your In-Laws

If your wife's parents are still around, this is will be traumatic for them. Nobody wants to see their children suffer like this so it's likely her parents will want to spend as much time with their daughter as possible. Regardless of what they want, you are the husband and your wife's primary family now. You'll need to set boundaries early on and communicate in your weekly check-ins how you're truly feeling about the situation.

Your wife will find it much easier to talk to her parents than you will, unless you have a close relationship with your in-laws, but if your wife doesn't know how you feel she won't know what to tell her parents. Ideally, her parents will recognise if they are shutting you out and will give you space without having to ask. But again, this is as traumatic an experience for them as it is for you and they won't always be thinking straight.

Your Own Extended Family

Your family members will find this traumatic as well, especially if they love your wife as a part of the family. As such, you can expect they will want to spend as much time with you and your wife as possible. Sometimes it might be difficult for your family to understand why you aren't visiting or calling as often anymore. By inviting them to see your new daily routines first-hand, they will be more understanding and offer ways they can help.

It was always great when my mother would visit because I could talk to her about issues I couldn't always discuss with Natasha or her parents, and my mother could see for herself how hard the situation was for us.

Siblings

If you or your wife have siblings, they will likely be a great support. They will be a similar age and may not be as traumatised as parents will be. My brother Trent helped give me some physical respite as he had the same strength as me to lift Natasha, which our parents didn't have. This meant I could take a break physically, which I desperately needed at times. I was able to do fun activities with my siblings at times and you might find they help take your mind off your difficulties.

When Family Is Too Much

Although support from families is great, sometimes this support will become too much. Your wife might feel your family is spending too much time with you but could be reluctant to raise this because she can see they are supporting you. You can ask her proactively whether she is happy with the situation and tell her you're willing to set boundaries with your family if that is what she wants. You don't want to add stress to an already-tough situation. You likely need time to yourselves so come up with creative ways of building that time into your life.

There are so many aspects to manage with this journey so be easy on yourself and comfortable with the mistakes you make along the way. You'll rarely manage all situations perfectly, especially the emotions of so many other people, but as long as you keep the focus on making your wife comfortable, you'll generally head in the right direction.

EXERCISE: DEALING WITH EXTENDED FAMILY

How are you feeling about your and her extended family situation? Are they too much? Do you need more help?

How can you find out how they are feeling about the situation?

How can you raise any anxieties with your wife, and check if she is feeling the same or differently to you?

KEY POINTS FROM PART 6

- Open and regular communication with your wife will help you avoid making assumptions about how each of you are coping and will bring you closer together.

- The most reliable method of helping you communicate with one another is to implement a weekly relationship check-in, which can be confronting for both of you at first, but you'll soon learn to enjoy the process.

- Emotions will run high during this journey. Developing patience and not taking anything personally will help you avoid reacting negatively.

- Your sex life will likely be affected by the cancer. Ensure you discuss this openly and try exploring other methods of being intimate.

- Try to involve children with the journey if you have them. Be open with them and check in regularly with their questions and fears.

- Having extended family around can complicate matters, because there are more emotions to deal with, but you can lean on them for support. Keep discussing with your wife about what is and isn't working, and experiment.

- If you're both struggling, there are marriage counsellors who are experts at helping you in these situations. Prevention is always better than cure.

PART SEVEN

END
OF LIFE

In this part I help you prepare for
the end of life if the worst does happen.

7.1

The Final Diagnosis

"I would have to learn to live in a different way, seeing death as an imposing itinerant visitor but knowing that even if I'm dying, until I actually die, I am still living."
- Paul Kalanithi MD, When Breath Becomes Air

I sincerely hope you will never need this part of the book, that your wife goes into remission and you never have to confront the prospect of her dying from cancer. Because of this, and because I want you to remain optimistic as a carer, I have left out any references to the possibility of your wife dying until now. It would be a miracle if every man reading this book sees their wife go into remission and live a long life, but there will tragically be many wives whose cancer is too advanced. This part of the book tells you what you need to know about this aspect of being a cancer carer if the bad news does arrive. I will cover how to make end-of-life plans, how to talk with your wife about this, and some advice for dealing with your grief.

Coming To Terms With The Final Diagnosis

If your wife's doctor has already told you the end is approaching, then you know this already: nothing can prepare you for the reality of hearing the news. Until this point, you have focused on being a carer and husband but you're now facing the reality of never seeing your wife again. You would think that because you might have been dealing with the cancer for a long time, you would be ready for this but something, call it survival instinct or cognitive dissonance, shuts us off from facing up to the reality that many cancers can be terminal. This instinct served you well when you needed to shut off the thought of losing your wife and focus on caring. Now, however, you must face a tragic reality.

It's easy to dismiss the news from your wife's doctor. You've both been fighting the cancer and yet your wife has still pushed on. So why wouldn't she do that now? Surely the doctors are wrong, or maybe this time the cancer will be cured. These are brave thoughts but will be ultimately unhelpful. Oncologists see a lot of death and know the signs well, so when they tell you that life is coming to an end, they are likely to be quite certain of it. They know what the machines are telling them, what your wife's body responses are telling them, and what all the statistics tells them.

Your job, when the experts tell you your wife's body is shutting down, is not to push away the thoughts, but to step up into the next phase of being a spouse cancer carer: preparing for a good death. You don't want any regrets after your wife passes away. It's far better to have prepared well for her death by spending time together and saying everything that needs to be said rather than to be sorry you were in denial and masked your fears.

You're the one who has to live on after your wife passes away so take responsibility for ensuring this phase goes as well as possible.

If your wife does miraculously go into remission - even after the doctors thought her life was ending - then know that following the advice in these chapters will never be a waste of time.

How Your Wife Might React

Chances are good that your wife will already know her body is shutting down, well before the doctors communicate this, which makes getting the news that much easier for both of you. It's made especially easier is if she has come to terms and is at peace with what will happen.

On the other hand, this will be a scary diagnosis for your wife. All that fighting and effort she has put in is now coming to an end with a feeling of defeat. She is now facing the prospect of never seeing this world again. Never to see you, her friends, her children (if you have them) or any of the beauty in this world. She can never go to her favourite restaurant again or do anything she loved to do.

Ernest Becker, in his Pulitzer Prize-winning book *The Denial of Death*, tells us that what people fear most is death but that we repress this fear so we can get on with our life. Now your wife can no longer repress this fear and must come face-to-face with the scariest feeling we could ever have as humans. People can react in unpredictable ways when dealing with the notion they are dying. Your wife might get short-tempered, become distant, depressed, or go into complete denial of her reality.

Your Job Is To Be Steadfast

St Paul, in his famous *Letter to the Corinthians* in the Bible, tells us that love is patient and kind. We normally think of patience as being passive and fatalistic. Interestingly, the word Paul originally used translates more accurately as *steadfast* instead of *patient*. In the face of suffering, which occurs in all loving relationships, you must remain steadfast in your goal, which is to give your maximum amount of love and care to your wife. You're likely to be physically and emotionally exhausted, but you must remain steadfast for her to truly enjoy the last moments she has with you here on earth.

Sweeping the reality of your wife's impending death under the rug - or denying anything is wrong - won't stop her from dying and will only make those final days and hours unnecessarily difficult.

How To Communicate The News To Other Family And Friends
You may well find that family and friends react in a worse way to the final diagnosis than you and your wife do. You've seen your wife every day so her deterioration probably is not a surprise. But for those who have not seen her recently, or were under the impression your wife was stable, this news can come as a real shock. They might go through the same feelings and reactions discussed above.

Your role here is to shield your wife from their reactions. Take over the role of sharing the news so she can conserve her limited energy. Ask her who she wants you to tell, and what she wants them to know, in the same way you've approached communicating with your supporters.

If you know your family and friends are not coping well, then tell them you don't need to deal with their emotions, but instead for them to support you and to help your wife have a good death. You have your own emotions to deal with, let alone trying to comfort those around you, which will add to your exhaustion and anxiety. You can advise family and friends to see counsellors to help them come to terms with the news so that when they do come to visit, they can do nice things like share happy memories and say a proper goodbye.

You might find many are in denial that this is the end, particularly if your wife's parents are still alive, because no parent wants to die after their children. Although it might seem stoic to 'rise above' the emotions of this stage of life, denial can lead to complications later. They won't have had time to process their emotions and say goodbye, which can lead to guilt and complicated grief when your wife does die.

If you notice this happening, you can discuss their reactions with your wife if she is up to it or ask a counsellor at the hospital or hospice to help out. They will have seen everything, good and bad deaths, and what they want most of all is to give your wife a good death. They are experts at this and will step up to help so you can focus on spending time with your wife.

How To Manage Visitors If There Are Too Many Of Them

In some cultures it is normal to have plenty of people around at the time of a person's death. Other people just want some quiet time with their loved one, which can sometimes be difficult. It can become stressful with too many people wanting to visit you and your wife when they hear the news that her life is ending. Visitors can be great but too many of them can disrupt the peace and drain your energy. Your job right now is to be the voice and strength for your wife. She won't have the energy to coordinate her family and friends and tell them when a good time to see her is.

This will change anyway as one moment she might want to see someone and the next she will want time alone without you in the room. If family and friends arrive but your wife is sleeping or doesn't want to receive them, try to explain calmly what the situation is. They will hopefully understand, but some might be distressed that they cannot see your wife. Assert control here. You know your wife better than anybody else so you are the ultimate judge of what is best for her. At first, being this assertive may be difficult and some people might resent you for it, but your primary focus is on making your *wife* happy, not them. Ideally you'll know in advance whether they intend to travel to visit, and you can ask your wife whether this is okay before they spend the time and expense to get there. I had some friends travel quite a long way only to find that Natasha didn't want to see anyone at the time and that I needed to spend time with her which meant I could only spend a little time with them. They understood the situation but it was disappointing for all of us. Of course, if they have pre-arranged a visit your wife may still change her mind later on – her feelings are unpredictable.

It's a great idea to have the company of your own loved ones at this time. Invite them over but don't let them drain your wife's energy. You can keep them outside and talk to them away from the room. Your needs right now are just as important. Maybe a family member can sit with your wife while you get a break and collect your emotions. As always, check with your wife about what she wants and trust your gut instinct about the right decision. A rational decision will be almost impossible to make but your heart will usually know what is right. My family spent a lot of time with me towards the end so they could support me practically and emotionally, as well as be close to Natasha, who I had been with for nearly eleven years by then, and was very much a part of our family.

EXERCISE: RESPONSE TO THE FINAL DIAGNOSIS

Ask yourself how you are feeling upon hearing of the final diagnosis. Maybe you want to write this down.

How is your wife feeling?

What is going to be difficult going forward (e.g. too many people coming to see her; how are you going to communicate with your wife?) and can you write down a simple plan for dealing with these difficulties?

Having dealt with these immediate reactions and advice for dealing with them, let's now take a step back and look systematically at everything to consider about this stage of life.

7.2

End Of Life Plans

"A paradigm shift of viewing palliative care or hospice as a gift instead of seeing it as giving up has the potential to change the way we experience advanced age."
- Lisa J Shultz, A Chance to Say Goodbye

This book has covered the power of planning and research extensively and now you need these tools more than ever. Everything can deteriorate quite quickly and you won't have the time to make plans or conduct research when your head is in a million places at once. So treat this preparation as a gift to your future self who will thank you for stepping up and doing the hard work earlier.

An end-of-life plan is vital to ensure your wife, her doctors and you are all on the same page. The plan is a document that details all of your wife's wishes for the end of her life. This focuses on the medical care but covers financial plans and lifestyle wishes such as funeral plans as well. It is different to a will as a will doesn't go into medical plans and is legally binding, whereas the end-of-life plan is more of a guide and plan for all considerations before death.

When your wife is referred to palliative care, the doctors will advise you when to fill out the plan and will give you a template with questions to follow. In this chapter I won't be advising you on what to complete, as this is deeply personal, but rather about how to go about the process as a couple, as it's far from easy. The conversations I had with Natasha about her end-of-life plan still feel like they happened yesterday. There is no easy way to go about this process but it's a process that must be done.

Although the doctors have asked you to fill this form out, it doesn't mean the end of your wife's life is imminent. Natasha survived a further four months after completing hers. It's impossible to know exactly when the end of your wife's life will be, therefore: 1) Don't put off doing the plan hoping you won't need to confront the process, and 2) Having the plan done will mean you can set it aside and forget about it until the doctors need it. You can rest assured you have talked everything over together and then get on with living your life as fully as possible. Decisions are hard enough to make on your own, especially when you're exhausted from a lack of sleep and emotional fatigue, so knowing the decision is already made, and was done so in collaboration with your wife when she was alert, is a major sense of relief.

Take Your Time And Research
If you're working out the end-of-life plan when your wife is still alert and not on the cusp of death, then you can afford to take your time to work out what is best. There's no rush. Even if you don't complete the whole plan, at least having discussed everything will give you peace of mind to know what your wife wants.

You can do your research and talk to people for advice. Ask your wife's oncologists about their recommendations and what to expect at the end of life. Talk to nurses about what they have observed works well and what goes wrong. Read books on how to have a good death. I personally recommend *Death, A Love Project, a guide to exploring the life in death and finding the way together* by Annie Bolitho.

Counsellors at the hospital or hospice can give you legal recommendations as well as ideas to prepare you for a good death. Some great advice I received from a hospice counsellor was to give Natasha things to hold and read that I could hold onto after she died knowing she had touched them. I gave her photos to hold as we talked about the memories, and our prayer books, which I still use.

Talk Openly With Each Other

Be prepared to have multiple conversations with your wife because sometimes the emotions will take over and you won't get to discuss the finer details. Maybe some questions will trigger stories you want to share so let that happen naturally without an agenda. There is no rush with this process. This is precious time you have together. Natasha and I each took our time to think separately about what was best, and then came together to discuss. This was a painful process for us as Natasha told me, "James, my friends are all filling in birth plans, and here we are filling in end-of-life plans."

If you have children, ask your wife how she wants her children to remember her and whether she wants them near her when the time comes. Maybe she wants to record a video for them or write some letters they can read. No matter what she looks like or how sick she is, she will want them to remember she loved them. But there may be times she doesn't want her children to see her, such as right at the end of her life or when she is in excruciating pain. If you have a different opinion, raise this respectfully with your wife, but ultimately you must do what she is comfortable with and respect the choices she is making when fully alert.

Make Or Update Your Wife's Will

Ideally you've already made a will early in your marriage, but many – like Natasha and I – did not. A will can be done quickly, with a lawyer helping you both with the process. Book in as soon as possible to get this done and, if you need the lawyer to come to you, then the extra cost will be a small inconvenience when you look back.

The other benefit of a will is that it puts down legally what your wife wants to have happen with her body, such as where she will be buried or if she wants to be cremated. This can be a vital tool if she has other family members who don't agree with her wishes and start fighting with you over this. You won't have the energy to fight anyone, nor will you want to try proving the conversations you had with your wife about where she wanted to be buried or what she wanted on her headstone.

Having a will ensures your wife's voice is heard even when she can no longer speak, either in an induced coma to relieve pain or after death. One of the few causes for contesting a will is that your wife was not of sound mind when making it, which is another reason for getting this done as early as possible when doctors and lawyers can all testify that indeed she was of sound mind.

If your wife dies without a will, this is referred to as dying intestate, and lawyers will divide up her estate according to the law instead of your wife's wishes. This can be an arduous process that requires publishing notices in newspapers to inform everyone about the process as well as finding and talking to lawyers at a time when you're grieving.

We didn't have wills as we were happy for each other to take charge of our assets, but in hindsight a will would have been far easier than having to prove our marriage to courts and hunt down her bank account details from multiple banks. There was so much back and forth and travelling around Australia to meet with lawyers as well as tight deadlines to meet.

Once The Plan Is Made, Forget About It

Now the plan and will is done, you can focus on the present knowing the future is taken care of. You know what the decisions will be because they have already been made. You can focus on having as good a time with your wife as possible, talking about happy memories and whatever you want to talk about. Don't bring up the end-of-life plan unless you need to, but after you've worked it out chances are it won't change.

Focus On Comfort And Dignity Rather Than Extending Life Unnecessarily

Hopefully, by this stage, if you're reading this chapter you've come to terms with the fact your wife's illness is terminal and you can focus on making the best choice for the end of her life. Almost every doctor will advise you to take an option if it is medically appropriate based on their expert advice, and if it won't cause pain and suffering. If all options are off the cards, and it's certain your wife is nearing the end of her life, you want this to be a peaceful death.

Natasha told me quite clearly that she didn't want resuscitation because if her heart stopped it meant her time was up. There was no point risking broken ribs, which can happen during resuscitation, and the pain for what might only be an extra day of living. She didn't want heroics like intensive care and painful tubes. In fact, when I asked the doctors about intensive care, they said they could easily do it but it would not be comfortable for Natasha because she would be under bright lights with lots of noise and we would not be allowed to visit. Is that how we wanted her to spend her final days?

Natasha had come to terms with her illness and knew that when her days were up there would be no point fighting unnecessarily. She told me to do what was medically appropriate and to talk to doctors about this, but mostly just to make her comfortable and to be there with her when she took her last breath. For her death, Natasha told me - and put down in her end-of-life plan - that she wanted to die in a nice environment, either at home or in the hospice, rather than in a hospital.

Consider Palliative Care
You might think palliation, the term for providing palliative care to a patient, is tantamount to giving up. Some people told me after Natasha died that I had given up on her but this is a common perspective on palliative care. You and your wife will make your own decisions, which might be different to ours. Talk to doctors about your wife's condition and spend time thinking about the possible scenarios. Go through different scenarios together and work out a good response to each one. You could visit the hospice and the hospital ward to see for yourself which one you would prefer. Research all the different options like intensive care and resuscitation. This is a major decision but one that needs to be done.

After talking with every doctor about all the possible options - including further radiation, intensive care, and having doctors on hand to resuscitate her - I made the big decision to take Natasha out of the hospital and back to the hospice, which is a medical centre focused on providing palliative care. All the doctors advised that this was the only medically appropriate path that would be peaceful and not risk further complications or drain her energy unnecessarily. At the hospice there was no noise and no rushing doctors and nurses. It was well away from the hospital. I could sleep in the same room as her. It was a beautiful environment in nature and close to water, and the hospice doctors and nurses were experts at pain relief. I have no regrets about how Natasha died, and this is important given I have to live the rest of my life with that decision. I am grateful for having our detailed end-of-life plans because I could confidently make decisions knowing what Natasha wanted for her life at this point.

Prepare For The Tough Process of Voicing The Decision To Doctors

Voicing end-of-life decisions will never be easy, even with a plan. A process to help with this is visualisation, which is similar to how a pilot trains for emergencies with simulators. When you have time on your own, spend a minute or two sitting comfortably and visualising talking about the plan with the doctors, so that when the real event happens your subconscious mind already knows what to do and how to react calmly.

EXERCISE: PREPARING TO DISCUSS END-OF-LIFE PLANS

- Before you talk with your wife about end-of-life plans, have a think about what you want for her end of life, with the following questions:

- Where would you like her to die, and where do you think your wife would like to die?

- Who do you want around her, and who do you think she wants around her?

- What do you need to have and do to give her the death she and you want?

- What are the options going forward as well as the pros and cons of each (e.g. intensive care and resuscitation)? Who can help you gain clarity on this? You can do your own research alone if you need to.

- Are you clear on what your wife wants at her end of life? Can you get clarity now instead of when everything is in turmoil?

- Visualise yourself voicing all the above decisions to the doctors. Think about where it might happen, who the doctors will be, how they'll ask you, what you'll say to them, and your emotions as you tell them. Sit with this visualisation until it feels real. This will make your life easier if this does become a real event.

I clearly remember the first time a doctor in the emergency room pulled me aside to ask me what Natasha's end-of-life plan was. I was shocked to hear the question and had to collect my thoughts. I knew what the plan was, but to voice it was one of the toughest things I have ever done. Nonetheless, despite Natasha being sedated, I was able to tell the doctors exactly what she wanted, which was a great relief.

I will never forget crying uncontrollably when I realised there was no other option except to make Natasha comfortable with palliation. I felt embarrassed at first but then comforted because the doctors let me cry, asked me how I was doing, how my antidepressants were helping, and reassured me I had been a great husband and carer for Natasha.

I felt so alone in that moment. Natasha's parents were with her in her room and my mother had left the previous day back to Tasmania, but it was the doctors who were there for me when I needed them in that moment. This is why building great relationships with them, as discussed earlier in this book, is so important not only for your wife's benefit but for yours too.

You're as much a part of this journey as your wife is, which is why this book is here for you. Your wife's suffering ends when she passes away, but you have to live the rest of your life without her. Preparing for a good death, although emotionally draining, is a gift both to her and to you.

7.3

The Final Conversations With Your Wife

"There are three things we have in life – energy, time and money, and I have run out of the first two of those."
– Natasha, two weeks before her death

Your wife will likely know when her time is growing short because she knows what her body is telling her and when it is shutting down. This is a time when she may bring up some questions she needs to talk about with you because they are on her mind and she doesn't want to die having not discussed them.

These questions will sometimes be difficult to answer and they will often take you by surprise. Your wife is not trying to catch you out. Rather, she wants to talk about these things as they come up for her. This is her way of saying goodbye and having the time to do so can be seen as one of the blessings of cancer compared to a sudden death where you don't have time to discuss all that's on her and your mind. This chapter is about helping you understand why she will ask certain questions and to help prepare you with some answers.

Never Sweep Away A Question

When your wife's health starts deteriorating, you gain a bit more certainty that her life will end soon. At the same time you still don't know exactly when she will pass away. My advice is this: If your wife brings up a topic, you mustn't sweep it away. This might be the only time you get to discuss that topic. The fact she has brought up it up means she is ready to talk about it, and you can be sure she has thought long and hard about preparing herself to ask the question. You don't want to avoid the question or try to 'lighten the mood' by laughing her question off. Your wife cares about you, loves you and wants to know about your life without her. She wants to know you'll be okay.

What follows are some of the questions she might ask and some of the underlying reasons why she is asking them. Your wife will have her own reasons and rather than assume, you can always ask what she wants to know.

Will You Be Okay?

Your wife might ask if you will be okay after she has passed away. No, you won't be okay and your wife knows this. She is saying many things with this question and most of all her question is an apology she cannot be there with you. She wants to know you will look after yourself and not become an alcoholic or self-destructive. She wants to know you'll see a doctor and be around friends and family. That you will miss her and you'll find it almost impossible to cope with life without her around.

Some responses you can try: "I'll stay healthy and fit, and get help when I need it," "I will have a hard time adjusting, but will work and have money to care for myself," "Although I'll work it out, life will never be the same." Yes, you'll be flattering her with this last response, and your wife will know it, but she will for sure love knowing your life will never be as good, easy or fun as when she was around.

Will The Children Be Okay?

Like all of these questions, it is impossible to know the future. You don't know if you'll be okay, let alone the children. She wants to know what you will do to look after them. Most of all, she wants to know they will still be loved without her around.

Here are some possible responses; "I will find as much help as possible. If my parents are still around, they will help, and if your parents are around, they will help too," "I will look into childcare options if I need to work and they are too young for school," "Our friends will step in to babysit or pick them up from school with their children," "I'll read our children stories, learn how to plait their hair, make their favourite food, and give them enough love for both of us," "I'll always share memories about their mum and keep your photos around so it will be impossible to forget you."

Will You Re-Marry?

You can never know if you will re-marry so it is difficult to tell your wife that you aren't thinking about it right now, while assuring her that even if you did re-marry it wouldn't change your love for her. Just as you never expected to find the woman of your dreams in her, who knows if you'll find another woman who makes you happy? With billions of women in the world, the chances are high. But this isn't the answer she wants to hear, and nor does she need to hear it. She wants to believe she will be the only woman you ever love, and you'll never look at another woman. Think about it in the reverse: you probably wouldn't want to imagine your wife being happy with another man if you passed away, even if you knew he made her happy and cared for her.

Tell her things like, "You make me so happy I cannot imagine being happy with someone else, and I love you with all my heart" or whatever works for you. This is true in the moment you tell her this, even if you do end up with someone else after she is gone. You're not lying to her, just telling her what is true at this moment.

When Natasha asked me about re-marrying, she wanted to know if I would be happier with someone else than with her, especially if I was able to have children with another woman. I told her that of course I wouldn't be happier, that even if there was another woman, my love for her wouldn't change, that I would never forget her, and that nothing can compare to what we had together. This is true. Relationships cannot be compared.

Will You Remember Me And Us?
You'll never forget your wife. You've been married, which means you know each other's most intimate secrets. You can never forget someone who means so much to you, even if you marry another woman later. But don't brush off this question. She's asked it because it's important to her.

You can tell her you'll remember her in so many ways by talking to her, praying to her or writing to her, visiting her grave, watching videos of you and her together, hanging photos of the two of you, spending time with the friends you shared, spending time with her family, talking about her with everyone, and by keeping some of her favourite clothes around.

When You Don't Have An Answer To Her Questions
It's fine to say you don't know the answer to a question (for example, will you be okay?). You could ask if you can have some time to think about her question or ask what exactly she would like to know. Even if you do have an answer, and then later think of

a better one, you can come back with it. You might want to write an email or a letter for her to read as you can say everything you want to without any interruptions or emotions getting in the way.

If you're stuck with an answer, which is understandable because you'll be exhausted, you can always fall back on talking about all of your favourite memories together, which you should spend time doing anyway, and she will never get tired of hearing how lucky you feel having been loved by her. Tell her how much you love her and how you have grown from this journey caring for her in ways you never thought possible, and that it's made you a stronger man.

My Experience Of These Conversations With Natasha

There was a time, two weeks before Natasha died, when we were sitting in the hospice after we had breakfast together, looking out over the lake. Natasha said to me, "James, there are three things we have in life – energy, time and money, and I have run out of the first two." Let me tell you, I had no idea how to respond! What do you say in that situation? Well, at least we have money? I soon realised she was telling me indirectly that her time was up and we needed to say goodbye. I must admit that I didn't give great answers to the questions Natasha asked me, which were most of the questions we explored above, and some were truly ordinary! But they were the best I could muster at the time with my exhausted physical and emotional energy. And that is enough - just to have that time to talk.

It helped me to remember some advice given to me as a beginner teacher, that my students would remember some of what I taught them, but mostly they would remember how I made them feel. So, focus less on what you're saying and more on the only thing your wife wants to know; that you love her and always will, and that you feel her love now and forever. She will care what you say, but mostly she wants to feel cherished and loved. This is what we are all after as humans; to be loved and to love others.

Nobody said this journey would be easy and, as it comes to an end, it doesn't get any easier. But do your best and speak from your heart. Try to tell her everything you want her to know so there is nothing left to say. Having these conversations will put her heart and yours at peace.

EXERCISE: THE FINAL CONVERSATIONS

Have a think about, or write in your cancer notebook, some answers to the following questions:

- What do you want to talk about in the final weeks with your wife?
- What do you absolutely need to say to her?
- What do you want her to say to you?
- How are you feeling about having these conversations?
- What are your answers to the questions in this chapter?
- If she doesn't ask you these questions, do you still want to give her the answers you've thought of? How will you raise these with her?

7.4

Dealing with Death and Grief

"Life is eternal; and love is immortal; and death is only a horizon; and a horizon is nothing save the limit of our sight."
- Rossiter Worthington Raymond

If your wife has passed away, then please know you have my deepest condolences. I understand your grief. You're feeling a wave of emotions right now and whatever you feel is okay. You will probably feel anger, sadness, disbelief and shock. You might feel relief, which will probably make you feel guilty, but nobody is judging you for the feelings you have. After the turmoil you've been through as a carer, it would only be natural to feel relieved. The truth is that you'll actually feel all these emotions, and sometimes all at once. This will be overwhelming because on top of all of this grief you have to work out what to do with your life now.

Your purpose and role as a husband and a carer is now over. This is a stark thought, because now what? Who are you if not these things? This can be an intense time of soul-searching. The worst part of this time is you don't have your wife to help you process it, which will lead to an intense feeling of loneliness. For all the time you've known your wife, nobody has known you as intimately as she has. She has witnessed all your quirks, struggles, joys, and emotions as your romantic partner. The very person you want to confide in and share everything with is no longer here, which is in turn the very reason for your struggles right now. It's a terrible feeling. This chapter will give you some practical tools to help you with these feelings after your wife's death.

Planning The Funeral According To Your Wife's And Your Wishes

Hopefully you were able to talk about your wife's funeral wishes or she wrote about these in her will. If not you can do whatever you want. You are her family so you get to decide how to celebrate her life. If you have children you can involve them in this planning too. This is what a funeral should be: a celebration of who she was, despite it being a sad memorial. If some people try to push their ideas and wishes onto you, take their suggestions on board but remember that this is your celebration of your wife's life. If you are truly stuck with ideas on how to make this a worthy celebration of your wife's life, there are experts who can help you plan a funeral.

The Timing Of The Funeral

Your exhaustion might mean that planning the funeral is the last thing you want to do, so you could consider delaying the funeral until you have the energy to make something special for her. Many people link the funeral to the burial and do both on the same day, but there are no rules with this. Maybe some religions or cultures have their own rituals but they were created by other humans and so can be changed by humans, that is, you. Rushing your friends and family to come over and inundate you right at your most intense period of grief, or rushing to prepare a memorial at this time, maybe isn't the ideal solution. One idea you could try is burying or cremating your wife in a separate ceremony, and then having a proper memorial/funeral later when you can make it truly what you want it to be, whenever you want to.

Your Wife Is Not Her Body
An objection to having a delayed funeral after a burial is that the casket with your wife's body won't be at the funeral. This connection to the body can be a reason people give for wanting the ashes or place of burial close to them so they can feel close to their loved one. Make a decision that feels right for you but my experience was that Natasha had two funerals. The first was with her body which was buried in the Philippines and the second back in Australia after the burial for all my family and friends as many couldn't make it to the first one. The second funeral was by far the more meaningful one to me, despite Natasha's body not being there, because I was the one who planned it and made it what I wanted it to be rather than rushing a funeral to be at the same time as the burial. This is what happened with the first funeral and all I remember is being in a daze the whole time; definitely not in the mindset to plan a special funeral.

Even though I went to Natasha's grave site in the Philippines every day for a week after the burial, I knew her spirit wasn't there so I felt little connection to her at that place. Instead she is always with me in my heart and living through me because of who she helped me become during our marriage. This to me is a more intimate way of remembering her.

Talk To A Therapist To Help With Your Grief
After the funeral and burial is over, you now have to focus on dealing with this intense grief you're feeling. Many people will have advice for you at this time. Every one of those people means

well and wants the best for you. Sometimes their advice will help and other times you want everyone to go away.

Unless someone has lost their spouse to cancer, they won't know what you're going through even though many will be empathetic and compassionate. Maybe they have lost their parents or friends, in which case they will understand grief, but losing a spouse is different. For this reason talk to a professional, whether it's a GP, therapist, grief counsellor, priest or all of them.

Professionals are trained to deal with difficult times in someone's life, so it makes sense to seek their help right now. Maybe you need some antidepressant medication, psychology, or grief counselling. Your doctor will help you through this time so ensure you see them as soon as possible. Find a psychologist who specialises in grief using the same tactics taught to you in Part 3: go to a clinic with multiple therapists and tell them what is going on so they can help find the right person to match you with. Ideally your GP will recommend someone good for you but not all doctors are great at dealing with mental health problems.

Grief Counselling Can Really Help
Grief counselling can be done individually or with a group, and you can find places nearby that have sessions you can join. In some countries this is subsidised or fully paid-for by the government. The counsellor is usually not a fully qualified psychologist but they have usually been through grief themselves and will have done a course on counselling. I had never done group therapy but surprisingly found it to be one of the few activities I looked forward to in my week. Group therapy helped me know I wasn't alone in how I was feeling, or in my struggles with dealing with life without Natasha. In fact, despite not going through that counselling any longer I still keep in touch with my group and we will go out for

dinners together. Like everything, you may or may not click with the group and/or the counsellor so only do things that help you rather than drain you even more.

Avoid Self-Destructing

In these times after losing your wife it will be tempting to do things that in the moment feel better but that you know for sure won't be good in the long run. I'm talking about using alcohol or non-prescribed drugs, or meaningless sex, or binge eating. We all know these activities are only done to numb the pain but in turn cause life to spiral downwards as they ruin our mental health. If you notice this happening, don't be hard on yourself. Just pick yourself up and go see your doctor. They will give you the right tools and prescriptions to get you out of this. You're not alone. There is amazing help out there waiting for you. Men are experts at bottling emotions up and pretending everything is okay, but it's a sign of weakness rather than strength to bottle emotions up and pretend. Strong men realise they need help and go out and get help to solve the problem head on rather than being weak and imagining the problem isn't there.

It can be tempting to bottle your feelings up if you feel nobody knows what it's like to go through what you are going through, but that doesn't mean they cannot help. Many of my friends told me they would help however they could as long as I told them what I needed. They are not mind-readers so cannot be expected to know how to help you if you don't tell them. Reach out and tell them you want a walk or a chat or ask if you can come over for dinner. You'll be pleasantly surprised.

If you need immediate help, call a helpline. Most countries have these provided for by the government or funded by donations. It could be a general helpline, one specifically for men, or one specifically for grief. I had used the general one during Natasha's cancer, as I told you about earlier, but found the grief one helpful after Natasha died. They were able to listen and give me great advice whenever I needed it. The call only needs to be ten or twenty minutes, so even if you're with family or friends and missing your wife - or are triggered - you can duck into another room, talk about how you're feeling with an expert, and then re-group and come back to the gathering.

There are many ways you can cope with the grief and there is no one right way. You must go on this next stage of the Hero's Journey in a way that makes sense to you. You might have what seem like silly ideas for coping when they come to you, but if you go into your grief with an open mind you'll find something that works for you. Maybe you write your wife an email or a letter or go to her favourite restaurant or put her clothes in a nice section of your wardrobe. Whatever works for you, just do it. You can always do something different later.

Final Thoughts
You'll find your whole identity has shifted from being a husband and carer to being a widower, which will be overwhelming and can feel impossible to deal with. Don't lose hope and know you will get through this, just like you dealt with the shift to becoming a carer when this was all new to you.

There is no timeline on grief. You don't have to rush your grief or feel you're taking too long to process it. Some will adapt quicker than others to this new way of life, so it is important not to judge yourself.

Finally, grief never goes away. Even if you eventually re-marry you won't suddenly be absolved of grieving for your wife. The grief will keep coming up at different points of your life and grief doesn't go away or get smaller, but you get better - over time - at living with it.

EXERCISE: YOUR LIFE AFTER YOUR WIFE'S DEATH
- What do you really want to have happen at your wife's funeral?
- Do you want to wait a bit before having the funeral, even if it means not having the body there?
- What options (e.g., grief counselling, medication) are you going to look into to help you? What are your next steps for exploring these options?
- How will you avoid self-destructing? Do you need to take alcohol out of the house?
- Who can you call in an emergency? It could be hotlines or a family member or friend.
- What will you do if you notice your focus at work slipping? Do you have enough savings to take time off work? Can you get government assistance?
- What sort of things could you try when the pain is too much? Writing to her? Going for a walk?

KEY POINTS FROM PART 7

- Hopefully, you never need this part of the book but if you do know that there is such thing as a good death and you can prepare with your wife for this moment.

- Talk to the professionals around you about the end of your wife's life and ask how they can help you and your wife.

- Be open to talking about difficult topics with your wife if she raises them, or if there is something you want to discuss with her. You don't want to have any regrets about anything left unsaid.

- Your job is to manage communication and visits from family and friends as well as you can. Gauge your wife's energy levels and protect her from unnecessary stress.

- Take time to make end-of-life plans that your wife and you are comfortable with. Research as much as you need to. Put the plan aside and forget about it until it's needed. The plan may never be needed, but at least you can be comfortable knowing that even in the worst situation you'll know exactly what your wife wants you to do.

- Make the funeral exactly how you want it to be. Don't worry about social norms or family pressures. If you need time before you have the funeral, know that it's okay not to have the body at the service in order to celebrate her life. Her spirit is no longer in her body anyway.

- Get as much help as you can and go deep with the grief rather than putting it off. There are many resources out there to help you so try them and see what works for you.

- Take your time with your grief and don't have any expectations. Grief can be unpredictable, but this is okay.

PART EIGHT

THE HERO IS CHANGED FOREVER

In this part you'll see how you change forever in every aspect of your life in ways you could never expect as you have gone through this journey.

8.1

The Second Half of Life

"So get ready for some new freedom, some dangerous permission, some hope from nowhere, some unexpected happiness, some stumbling stones, some radical grace, and some new and pressing responsibility for yourself and for our suffering world."
- Richard Rohr, Falling Upward: A Spirituality for the Two Halves of Life

Here we are in the final part of our journey together. It has not been an easy one and you've had to deal with many tough issues. You've built new tools, gotten rid of habits that weren't working, and developed a whole new understanding around your purpose as a champion carer and husband. You've deconstructed and re-created your marriage too. Congratulate yourself for reaching this part of the story. I congratulate you.

This part of the story is unexpected. The story that most people expect is that it will be all bad and that there's no hope. This part of the book is all about the goodness and strength you've developed over the journey with your wife. That journey might still be going for you. It might be coming to an end or it may have already ended. Wherever you are, because of what you've been through or are still going through, you've become a true champion. A Heroic husband and carer.

It's this part of the Hero's Journey where you go back to the normal world a changed man. Everything has changed for you, and sometimes you'll feel as though you're living in a whole new world. Only it's not the world that changed; it's you.

There is new research being published about a concept called post-traumatic growth. You might have heard of the concept of post-traumatic stress disorder (PTSD) but the idea of growth after trauma might be new. I first learned about post-traumatic growth in Sheryl Sandberg and Adam Grant's book *Option B* and when I too experienced how my journey with Natasha had fundamentally transformed me forever, I knew I had to write about how you too will change from it.

I will cover some of the major aspects of your life that have probably changed the most for you. Some of them might not seem like big changes but they are. Other changes you might not feel yet because you're still in the midst of everything. In fact, changes might take many years to feel the effects of. But there will be change, and this is something to be hopeful about.

A crisis in life will shake your core in ways you cannot imagine. You've succumbed to a major crisis in having your whole life disrupted, so it seems natural that your life following this crisis will be different to how it was before. I had no idea this would happen and thought I would step back into the way life was before. In fact, when Natasha asked me what would be next for me when she passed away, I said I would go back to work. This seemed logical - that everything would fall back into place like a stretched elastic band.

But here's the catch: an elastic band doesn't go back to where it was before. It's been stretched and cannot go back to how it was. It's like what happens to a country after the most severe tsunami has ravaged it. You cannot un-crisis your life. Its aftermath is a part of you forever.

A friend gave me a book after Natasha died entitled *Falling Upward* by Catholic priest Richard Rohr. It's a short book yet it gave me the greatest comfort, which is why I'm sharing its lessons with you. Rohr tells us that most people will have a crisis, which will separate our lives into two parts. For most men, this can be seen as a midlife crisis which is a point when they realise they have been working and chasing money and career success, without much point beyond this.

A crisis shakes up everything that someone thought was important and turns them toward the only thing that is important, which is living a life full of love. Your second half of life, whether it's with your wife in remission or without her after death, will be different to the first. Your mindset will have shifted and your life will never be the same. Before the crisis, I was focused on money, getting a house, working my way up the career ladder, and becoming famous. I thought these would make me happy because society tells us that is the recipe for happiness.

I wanted to start a global company, be invited to do a TED talk and buy fancy cars. But now I'm a changed man in my second half of life. I still have strong ambitions but they are no longer about me. My goal is to serve others and help people live flourishing lives. I might make a lot of money doing this, I might not, but this no longer matters. My eyes have been awakened to realising what is truly important.

Some of the changes won't be clear at first. It took months to see how my life was new and years later I'm still discovering how the crisis has changed me. I will explore - in the following chapters - the many ways your life will be different, including your spirituality, relationship with yourself, relationship with your wife, and your capacity to change.

8.2

Rising Up From Being Broken

"You have to build calluses on your brain just like how you build calluses on your hands. Callus your mind through pain and suffering."
– David Goggins, Cannot Hurt Me

Nobody ever wants life to be hard. As humans we crave comfort. We want the temperature in our house to be just right. We want the food to taste the way we like it. We want our emotions to always be under control, and we long for safety. This is a deep human need, evolved over hundreds of thousands of years. To be confronted with danger is against every human instinct for survival.

Yet you have been thrown well outside your comfort zone and been broken and tested like never before. Few people experience this in their lifetime but as someone who has gone through one of the worst catastrophes imaginable, you are one of those people. Now, nothing can ever touch you. Bring it on!

You're unstoppable now. You know how far out of your comfort zone you can go and still survive. You will feel this in your own way. No longer will you be pushed around. You are your own man now. You've been broken. You've been tested. You'll begin to pity those who have not experienced hardship because they don't know how to live fully. They will be afraid of anything outside their comfort zone and choose a life that is nowhere near what they dreamed for themselves. You, however, can take on anything. Nothing compares to seeing your precious wife fight against death and rely entirely on your care and love. Nothing is this tough except going through the illness yourself. Yet you've taken on the challenge and stepped up. You'll never be the same.

A Tool To Rise Up From Suffering

Barry Michels and Phil Stutz teach many powerful psychological tools in their book *The Tools.* Here I want to introduce you one of my most-used tools of theirs called The Tower. The power of this tool is you can turn your life from being a victim into being infinitely powerful. If you let the pain have power over you you are held back from living your fullest life. You will need to use some visualisation for this tool but don't worry if this doesn't come easily to you. With a bit of practice you can learn to use this tool easily.

1. Imagine yourself at the bottom of a dark tower. Think of a moment when you've suffered, and then let this pain kill you in your imagination. See yourself at the bottom of the tower (first or third person, it doesn't matter), stone dead from this pain.
2. Now, hear a voice calling you from the top of the tower telling you that "Only the dead survive." As you hear this, you feel a burst of energy in your heart and that is connected to a bright light at the top of the tower.
3. You immediately come alive and the light pulls you out of the tower into the infinite light above it. You've transformed your pain into power.

4. Try the exercise again but this time as soon as you feel the pain and the death, immediately feel the light and rise up. This way you re-wire your mind to associate that moment of pain as a moment of strength and rising up rather than being a victim of it.

5. Repeat the tool as often as you need until you no longer see the moment of pain as pain but rather a gift that made you stronger. A warning, though: this tool is so powerful it can exhaust you if you use it too often to begin with. Also, if the pain is intense, the light might not be strong enough to pull you out of the tower. This is normal. Keep repeating the tool until you get out.

I now try to remember to do this anytime I feel pain, whether due to a present issue or a past memory. Maybe when I make a mistake at work, receive negative feedback, or whenever I feel the grief of losing Natasha holding me back.

All of us feel pain, from small amounts to full crises. But what separates exceptional people from victims is they let the pain make them stronger. Because that is what pain does if you allow it to. Instead of staying at the bottom of this dark tower in our minds, instead transmute the pain into power. This is what is meant by the term 'what doesn't kill us makes us stronger'.

The Japanese have a term for this, *kintsugi*, which refers to mending broken pottery with gold instead of throwing the pottery out. The scars are unique to each pottery piece as no two breaks will ever be the same. This is what makes the new pottery so much more beautiful. It has its own story on the way to perfection. Not only does the bowl or cup or vase still perform its original duty but it does so now with more beauty.

That is your life now: forever transformed by the pain, you now go forth to do your duty in a more beautiful way than you could ever have imagined possible.

8.3

You Will Value Time Like Never Before

"Live every day as though it is your last, because someday you will be right."
— Steve Jobs

Time is the most precious gift you have and once you use it up it cannot be regained. You have first-hand experience of the value of time because you've seen how much your wife would do to gain one extra day.

Most people live as though they will live forever. They forget about death because it's too scary a thought. But you've experienced death first-hand. Even if your wife makes it into remission, she has been fighting the real prospect of death. You now know death intimately. You know better than anyone how precious life is and that the human body is far from bulletproof. There will come a time when we all breathe our last.

And yet, almost everyone wastes the limited time they have here on earth working in jobs they hate, counting down until hump day and then Friday. They come home exhausted and look for entertainment on TV. They get drunk on the weekend to forget the week. They count down to when they can go on a holiday. They fill in every single spare moment not with precious thoughts but with social media and entertainment. As Jim Kwik tells us in his book *Limitless*, compared to the 15th century we now consume as much data in a single day as an average person from the 1400s would have absorbed in an entire lifetime.

The beauty of remembering you will die is that you are now free. Steve Jobs told us in his famous Stanford commencement speech to live every day as though it's our last because one day we will be right. This doesn't mean saying goodbye to everyone every day. It means living your life moment to moment in a way you will be proud of looking back. You are free to act knowing you have nothing to lose. That negative comment on your YouTube video? That potential client that chose not to use your services? None of it matters because the alternative was letting fear get in the way and not taking the risk at all.

Think of yourself in five or ten years in the future looking back at the choices you're making now. Will "future you" be proud or ashamed? Will you wish you had started that project back then? Will you be frustrated that fear held you back yet again and that you thought you had something to lose?

One of the silver linings of going through this crisis is you'll never again waste any time. Sure, there will be days you're exhausted and need to rest, but even that is not wasted time if the rest rejuvenates you to keep fighting. I spent a lot of time in bed after Natasha died, and sometimes drank excessively to numb the pain, but the exhaustion and pain eventually subsided as my new life started to take shape.

As long as you can live in a way that no matter when you were to die you would be happy with what you've done in your life, then you will always do justice to the battle you've fought alongside your wife.

8.4

Comparing
To Others

"You marvel and applaud big heroes in their big heroic actions, and forget you are a hero in your humble life and have modest heroic actions to complete yourself."
- Bangambiki Habyarimana

Your life is unique so comparing it to others is pointless, even though we all do it anyway. This will be another major change for you as you leave the Hero's Journey and come back to everyday life. You will often resent that you were the one who had to endure all this hardship while others were able to live a 'normal' life. You might be angry that your career has been affected. If your wife died, you'll be angry you no longer have your wife by your side.

I would often compare myself to everyone around me after Natasha died. I would see everyone going off to work, doing important things, while there I was there with barely the energy to get out of bed. I would chastise myself for being a lazy failure and thought to myself: "How dare I waste my time doing nothing and only simple things with my time when others are out there being productive?" I felt worthless. I would compare myself to my friends who had children and a happy marriage. I no longer had my wife and was struggling with depression. Why would I impose myself onto other people's happy lives? My sister was always out socialising with friends yet I didn't even have the energy to turn on the TV. "How boring you are, James!" I would think.

Eventually I realised that my life is my life and I'm not living for anyone else. Coming to this realisation took a lot of work with my psychologist and grief counselling group. In the group I was surrounded by people who were equally angry, upset and exhausted. They could deeply understand and empathise with what I was going through. I also began to realise that there are people in all sorts of difficult situations. Plenty of people are working at home, or don't have the energy they once had, or have lost their partners.

But it didn't matter if nobody else had my circumstances. I learned to accept my life situation as unique. Nobody else could ever be in my exact situation so why compare? Even people in my counselling group were in different situations to me. I needed to relax and know I was exactly where I needed to be. If I couldn't work then that was my reality, so I chose to resign from my job following Natasha's death. If I needed a day in bed because I was utterly exhausted, then I should do it knowing I was building up my energy for what was next. If I only wrote one sentence of this book instead of my goal of 500 words, then that was better than nothing.

Your life is *your* life. The way you re-enter the normal world after being through your Hero's Journey is unique to you and won't be like mine or anyone else's. Be at peace with this. Once you get used to being unique, you'll be free. You'll never again compare your car to your colleague's, your house to your neighbour's, your job to your sibling's, or your family situation to your friends'. You'll only compare each day to your yesterday, taking one step forward towards where you alone are meant to be. You'll make the choice to live *your* life, not the life *society* tells you to live. This is a lesson everyone needs to learn, but few do. Be grateful you've come across this lesson, albeit the hard way!

I had to redefine what I considered to be "normal". You'll do the same and realise your version of normal is like nobody else's, and this is okay. You are now free to redefine your life precisely the way you want to, according to nobody's rules but your own. As to comparing myself to people in suits going to work in Melbourne where I had moved to live with my sister? I eventually realised nine to five is actually not that fun, and everyone would be happy to have the time off I did. In fact many of my friends told me as much.

If you're worried about what people think of you, then know that actually people are not thinking about you as much as you think they are. Everyone has enough going on in their own lives as it is.

8.5

True Happiness

"I'm drawn across the universe to someone I haven't seen in a decade, who I know is probably dead. Love is the one thing we're capable of perceiving that transcends dimensions of time and space. Maybe we should trust that, even if we cannot understand it."
– Brand, Interstellar

We are taught in today's society that happiness comes from how much we own, our job title or how many places we have travelled to. Yet our gravestone will never list these out because people don't care about them. All they care about is how you made them feel; were you warm, loving, caring, and a good person?

A fancy car only has value because it's nicer than other cars. If there was only one type of car people could buy, then nobody would ever have a better car than someone else. True joy comes from loving ourselves and loving others. The love of your wife, or your children, or your friends: these are what will truly bring you joy and are literally priceless. There will always be someone else with more money than you, no matter how much you make. There will always be someone with a fancier job title no matter how much you are promoted. If you base your happiness on something that can only be compared to others, you'll never be satisfied.

There is a book entitled *Happy Money* by Elizabeth Dunn and Michael Norton that I recommend. Its message is that when we buy material things our happiness is quite high momentarily before going back down when that new thing becomes an old thing. Think of your smartphone when it's nice and shiny in the box: how happy did it make you when you first got it? How happy are you now with it? Material things will never make us truly happy, even if they make us happy in that moment of buying it.

What you'll learn in this journey with your wife is that love is all that matters. Love is not zero-sum or a competition; it's there for everyone to experience if you allow it. All that matters to your wife is how much she is loved and all you need to do is value her love for you.

You Will Love Like Never Before

This journey of yours will test your love like never before. It's easy to say "I love you" but love is about actions and not words. By pushing yourself to become a champion carer and husband in implementing the techniques and habits in this book, you'll be showing your wife precisely how much she is loved.

This love is something you'll carry with you for the rest of your life. If your wife enters remission, you'll know what it takes to show her how much she is loved. If your wife passes away, you'll feel her love and the power of loving her even when she is gone. This is one of the biggest changes in feelings as a result of this journey. I thought I loved Natasha before her cancer but becoming her carer made me love her even more. I had to wholeheartedly sacrifice my life for her and I realised what it actually means to love in sickness and in health. Sure, there were times I didn't have the energy to show my love, and times I forgot to show my love, and mistakes I made that could be construed as not loving her, but this is all part of it.

You'll never be perfect and you have to learn to love in a whole new way. But one of the blessings of this journey is that you get to learn about love in a way that other couples rarely get to. Your love will become stronger and more beautiful than it ever was before. This is true happiness.

Treating Others Well

Another change having gone on this journey is how you interact with others. You may have already done this well, which is great, but now you'll have a deeper understanding of other people.

You'll realise that everyone has their own struggles, no matter how normal they seem. Think of your own life. People who see you on the street will have no idea of what you've been through and are still going through. Even your friends might not know the details of your everyday life, yet you know intimately what sort of hell you're going through. Maybe even your wife had no idea how hard the journey was for you because you found it hard to tell her., just as you might not have known for sure about everything that was going on for her.

Everyone is going through something in their life. Social media makes it seem that others' lives are perfect, even though nobody has a perfect life. They might be dealing with a miscarriage or are finding it hard to get pregnant, or their children are not feeding or sleeping properly, or their boss is giving them a hard time, or their car has been broken into, or they are going through a divorce. That cashier at the grocery store might be a bit slow in scanning your items because his father was diagnosed with something yesterday. No matter what, everyone is going through something.

Because you know yourself how much pain you're hiding, you can now realise others are doing the same thing. You have a choice. Do you get upset with them or give them the benefit of the doubt? Do you assume the worst or the best in others? Can you shift your assumption to the idea that everyone is human and being human is hard?

You'll become an expert at understanding others, especially because of how often you are in hospitals, witnessing so much pain and suffering in others who might seem normal on the outside. This is a gift. Now you can truly empathise with others in a way few people can. You can help others or give them a smile; a shared understanding that everyone is going through something hard. This is how to live a life with true joy; joy that is more easily available to you having gone through this crisis. It doesn't make much sense but nothing about this journey does, does it?

8.6

The Tangible Growth Through Becoming A Champion Carer And Husband

"One can have no smaller or greater mastery than mastery of oneself."
- Leonardo da Vinci

Let's have a quick look at some of the skills you've acquired along this journey:

1. A growth mindset;
2. Extreme flexibility and embracing uncertainty;
3. Stoicism;
4. Overcoming perfectionism;
5. Overcoming your ego;
6. Courage;
7. Opening up and getting help from professionals, friends and family;
8. Mindfulness;

9. Self-care;
10. Communication;
11. Developing a sense of purpose in everything you do.

Let's look at these skills in more detail and how they apply to every aspect of your life going forward, not just as a husband and carer.

1.   A growth mindset

We all must grow in every aspect of our lives. If we stop growing we get comfortable and can never expand our horizons. You've experienced tremendous growth during this journey and have had to apply the growth mindset while always being open to learning new skills no matter your starting point. This is the opposite of a fixed mindset, where someone believes they are born with a fixed level of capability and cannot change. Nobody was born being able to be a champion carer and husband. You had to learn how to do this under extreme conditions. And you did. You refused to give up and pretend you could never learn how to do it.

EXERCISE: GROWTH MINDSET

Given how much you have learned on this journey, what else can you learn to do in your life more generally that you thought was out of reach before?

---

2. Extreme Flexibility and Embracing Uncertainty

Life requires flexibility in every facet. I believe humans are called to live our lives as fully as possible, which means stepping outside what is comfortable and predictable. Even in making plans for dinner, you need to be flexible. Trying to stay resolute and fixed to your plans is a recipe for disaster because most plans don't work out. Many people cannot handle this unpredictability of life so they reduce the boundaries of their comfort zone until they only have plans guaranteed to work out, such as doing the same things day in and day out. You didn't choose to have your life upended like it has been but you can be grateful because the upset has taught you how to live every single day with extreme flexibility. Now you can live knowing that no matter what happens, you can adapt and overcome.

EXERCISE: FLEXIBILITY AND UNCERTAINTY

What will you do with your power of being adaptable to whatever life throws at you? What has thrown you off balance in the past and would it do so now?

---

3. Willpower

Martin Seligman, the psychologist and author who helped start the positive psychology movement, demonstrates research showing that willpower predicts academic performance twice as much as IQ. The other exciting aspect of willpower is that it's something that can be developed whereas most people think it's a trait we are born with and cannot change.

You've required immense willpower at every stage of this journey, and if you didn't have any before, you had to develop it. Now you have that willpower, which will help you in everything you do.

EXERCISE: WILLPOWER

Whether it's using willpower to install new healthy habits, or to push through with job applications or starting a business, or even to work on new and existing relationships, how will this superpower serve you now?

---

4. Stoicism

You've experienced the ultimate lack of control throughout this journey. Almost everything was outside your control yet you made the choice to focus on those small aspects you could control. What you found was that there was a surprising amount still within your control and the more you focused on this the stronger you felt and the more self-esteem you had.

You will constantly experience things outside your control. In fact, as soon as you are dealing with any other person in your life, from your spouse to children to colleagues to employees to politicians running your country, there is so much outside your control. You cannot control their mood, how they will react to what you do or say, or whether a fellow driver is having a bad day and takes that out in the form of road rage.

Most people respond to this lack of control with a feeling of helplessness. They get angry at the news on TV, or they fight back when someone hurts them, or they give up on their dreams because everything is too hard.

You never had the option of giving up on this journey. Despite so much being out of your control you could not just lie there and let it be. You had to step up and control what you could. Your wife and your own well-being depended on this choice. Now you can live your life knowing what it takes to make this choice, knowing how to identify what you can and cannot control, and knowing the power that comes from choosing to control what you can control over the helplessness of trying to control what never could be.

EXERCISE: KNOWING WHAT YOU CAN AND CANNOT CONTROL

What in your life is out of your control and what is within it? Can you repeat this question every day to help you remain calm and focused?

---

5. Overcoming Perfectionism

We covered the dangers of a perfectionist mindset when talking about being the good enough husband instead of a perfect one. Perfect is the enemy of the good. You'll never even try anything if you set out only to be perfect, because perfection is impossible. You won't be the world's first perfect human and nobody will. You won't have the world's first perfect marriage. You won't be the world's first perfect caregiver.

But that's okay because you will instead be striving to be the best version of you: the best husband you can be, and the best person possible. You will fail at times, sometimes drastically, but you're trying your best. You'll notice yourself beginning projects you would never have even tried before, because you know the goal is not to be perfect. These projects might have seemed impossible before but that was because of your conception of them. If you think the only way to overcome them is without any mistakes and perfectly the first time, then of course the task will seem impossible. But now you know what it truly takes to be great. You know you won't be perfect the first time, or ever. You know you'll have to make mistakes. You know that as long as you try your best and improve every day, you will become a true Hero.

A Hero is not one who is perfect but rather one who knows what it takes and is willing to push through when they make mistakes in an effort to constantly improve.

EXERCISE: PERFECTIONISM
How can you apply this mindset to everything you do, including your health, work, projects, and relationships? What will you start doing that you were too afraid of in the past because you could never do it perfectly?

---

6. Mastering Your Ego

Your ego has created a sense of who you are, that you are a certain type of person because you have a certain education or a certain career, or how you look or think.

Throughout this journey you've had to dissolve your ego to become more self-aware. You've let go of everything you thought was important as you were fully of service to your wife. The ego hates this process of letting go and will normally do its best to resist it. You may have experienced this resistance if you found it difficult to identify as a carer, for example, because this is not the identity your ego has created.

But you've overcome that resistance and shown your ego who is boss. No matter what story it's created about who you are and what your education or job or upbringing means, you are able to change the story. You can treat all of this story as a collection of thoughts because that is all they are. You have chosen to insert new thoughts throughout this journey. When you let go of your past, you'll experience a beautiful sense of freedom.

EXERCISE: YOUR EGO

If this is all just a story, and you have the power to change the story and create a whole new one, what story will you create? What ideas will you have? What thoughts will you let go of and what will you insert?

---

7. Courage

One of the greatest superpowers a man can have is courage. Courage is needed to break free of your comfort zone and live the life you feel called to live. If you want a great job, high income, a good relationship, a bigger impact on the world, then all these dreams require difficult and scary steps.

In a way, then, you can be grateful for your experience of hardship. You've been thrust out of your comfort zone on a timeframe you didn't choose and have risen to that challenge with powerful courage. Now you can use this same courage to take the next leap, which will hopefully be on your own terms.

Antifragile is a word that I love, and it means that you are the opposite of fragile. Something fragile breaks when it is smashed, but something antifragile gets stronger. That's how you can choose to look at the suffering you have been through – it has made you antifragile with immense courage to fight anything.

EXERCISE: COURAGE

What will you do for yourself that previously seemed scary now that you have built up your courage through this journey?

---

8. Opening Up and Getting Help from Professionals, Friends and Family

Life will always throw up challenges and sometimes you will need help when facing those challenges. Maybe you have a challenge of leaving a job you hate or starting a new business. Whatever the challenge, you'll always need help with this. Humans are social beings and, although there is much you can do on your own, having help makes life that much easier.

Throughout this journey as a carer you've needed help from many people, and reaching out for that help has required humility, courage, open-mindedness and strength. By now you are becoming an expert in seeking help, even if only from your wife or your siblings.

EXERCISE: OPENING UP TO OTHERS

How will you open up to others when you need help in the future? Who can you call on?

---

9. Mindfulness

To be mindful is to live fully in the present, not worried about what's happening next, or what has already happened before. You had to learn how to do this, not in a fancy course or a trip to India but with real life shaping you on the journey. Every moment talking to a doctor, lifting your wife, communicating with her - these were all opportunities to practise mindfulness because if you let even something small slip there were often big consequences.

In today's world with infinite distractions, mindfulness is a superpower. You now have that power of focus and indistractibility.

EXERCISE: MINDFULNESS

How can you be mindful in your daily life? What will you be able to do with fewer distractions or anxieties about the past and future?

---

10. Self Care

You've had to learn how to care for yourself. Part 4 was dedicated to self-care and you quickly learned in this journey that if you didn't focus on self-care then everything else became even more difficult. If you didn't prioritise your health, sleep, energy management, relationship with your wife, or reaching out when life was hard, then you would find the journey much tougher. Nobody else was going to focus on these things for you either. It was up to you.

This ability to care for yourself will sow benefits in every aspect of your life. You'll put yourself first knowing this isn't selfish but rather how you bring your best self to your relationships, work and life.

EXERCISE: SELF-CARE

How can you care for yourself in your life even if you are no longer a carer?

---

11. Communication

You've had to communicate in the most difficult circumstances imaginable. Talking with doctors about the latest scans, talking to nurses in an emergency situation when everyone is exhausted, communicating bad news to friends and family, and having difficult conversations with your wife.

Great communication is a skill and few people are good at it. Most people will credit communications courses they took as finally teaching them this skill. I learned from Dale Carnegie's classic book *How to win friends and influence people* but even that masterpiece could not teach me in the same way this ordeal taught me.

Again, you can look at the journey you've been on with gratitude for having forced you into having the most difficult conversations you've likely ever had. You know you are now able to talk with others confidently knowing that few interactions will be as draining and difficult as what this journey has needed from you. You might pick up the phone for a sales call knowing that rejection cannot hurt you, or you might tell a family member their actions are dragging you down, or a boss that you are quitting.

EXERCISE: COMMUNICATION

What difficult conversations do you now feel confident about having that you didn't before?

---

12. Developing a Sense Of Purpose In Everything You Do

Finally, having gone through this journey you are now able to live a purposeful life. You know what it takes to live a truly meaningful life. The meaning you've found from this will be different for everyone but might include feeling a sense of purpose as a carer or as a husband. You may no longer see your life as material situations but rather as having a deeper meaning behind them.

When I first read Viktor Frankl's book *Man's search for meaning* it didn't make much sense. I had no idea how to find meaning in my life and it was easy to think that maybe life wasn't meant to have meaning. I bought random things and didn't think too much about making the most of my time. Now Frankl's message makes sense and I refuse to do anything in my life that doesn't match up with my own sense of purpose, whether it's work related, who I choose to build relationships with or what I spend money on.

When you live a life true to your unique purpose and your unique values, and when everything you do is connected to that, your life takes on a whole new expansive dimension.

EXERCISE: YOUR PURPOSE
What is your purpose in life? What are your values now? How will you change your life to align with those values and purpose?

It's plain to see precisely where the experiences of caring for your wife have led you to a new level of growth that would not have been imaginable before. Maybe it will take some time for you to experience this growth or to look back on the journey with gratitude, and that is okay. Maybe it takes many years to gain this perspective but have hope and the belief that perspective will come. The story I begin the next chapter with highlights this.

8.7

Your
Spirituality

*"We are not human beings having a spiritual experience.
We are spiritual beings having a human experience."*
- Pierre Teilhard de Chardin

Even if you don't follow a religion, you'll likely find yourself asking questions about whether there was a reason for the suffering inflicted on your wife and you. You'll often be told by well-meaning people that everything happens for a reason, which will become a frustrating phrase. We are all looking for something to make sense of what is happening to our lives. Sometimes you are so desperate for good news that even if you've never believed in God or a higher power, you find yourself praying anyway, just in case!

Even if you don't call it God, God is wherever you feel love. The love you have for your wife and the love she has for you. The love of your friends and family. The love of nurses and doctors.

This is God, or bliss, or true joy, whatever you want to call it. Unfortunately, we often require a great deal of suffering to unlock this love and joy.

I want to tell you a powerful story, adapted from Kamla K Kapur's book *Rumi: Tales of the Spirit: A Journey to Healing the Heart*, originally told by the sage Rumi over 800 years ago.

Ahmed was sleeping peacefully in an apple orchard when he was suddenly thrust wide awake. There was a big man in a dark cape whipping him with his horse whip.

"What are you doing?" "Why are you hitting me?" asked Ahmed, but the man didn't reply and just kept hurting him.

Ahmed was barely awake and thought this must be a nightmare, but the pain was too real to be a dream. The man would not stop.

Ahmed thought to himself that maybe he had done something wrong to deserve this punishment but could not remember ever hurting a man like this. He tried to run away despite the pain, but the stranger got back on his horse and easily kept up with him. Ahmed was exhausted and tried to sit under an apple tree, but from the top of his horse the man kept whipping him. Ahmed had no idea when the pain would end, if it ever would.

Then the man pulled out his sword and held it at Ahmed's neck. "Eat the rotten apples on the ground," he told Ahmed. "And don't stop unless I tell you to."
"What? Why?" asked Ahmed, but the man pointed the sword closer to his neck and started stuffing the rotten apples into Ahmed's mouth.

Ahmed wanted to ask the man who he was and why he was doing this to him, but he could not because he was so stuffed with apples and his mouth was full of them. Instead he tried to think back on all of his life and all the suffering he had gone through. He concluded that life is meaningless and full of suffering, with no point at all to it. He gave up trying to find any meaning and just accepted this fate.

At that moment, the man put away his sword and pulled out his whip again and started whipping Ahmed. "Run!" he screamed at Ahmed. "Run as fast as you can!" Ahmed was still sleepy, in incredible pain, and stuffed with apples. The last thing he thought he could do was run any more. But the whip was painful and he had no choice but to heed the man's demands.

All night Ahmed ran with the man on his black horse following him and whipping him to keep going. Finally, they came to a stream and the man made Ahmed bend down and drink from it. He was thirstier than he had ever been before and could not wait to drink the water. He drank, but when he had had enough the man whipped him and made him drink more.

He then sat back from the stream and uncontrollably threw up. All the apples and water came out and he felt like he would die in miserable pain and suffering. "This is all life is," he thought to himself. "We just suffer and then we die. That is all there is. We are not special and life has no meaning."

He turned to the stranger, who had gotten down from his horse. Ahmed thought this was the end so he said to him, "Please just kill me with your sword. I have no energy to resist. But first, please tell me why you have done this to me."

The stranger pointed his sword to the vomit in front of Ahmed. There, amongst all the rotten apples lay a long black snake still alive and hissing. The man put his sword away, placed his hand on Ahmed's shoulder and explained to him, "I was riding past you on my way to the next town, when I saw you sleeping. At that moment I saw that snake slither into your open, snoring mouth."

"But why didn't you just wake me and tell me this? I would have done everything you told me to and would even have eaten those apples and drank all that water and suffered your whipping if I knew there was a reason behind it."

"Because," the stranger replied to him, "if I had told you there was a black snake inside of you, you would have died of fright. This was the lesser suffering. Now you are free."

Ahmed turned and hugged the stranger, thanking him profusely. "Thank you for saving me, for giving me this freedom, for knowing what suffering I needed to live!"

I love this story because it helps make sense of the suffering you've gone or are going through. The strength, courage, resilience and love you now have could only come from this level of suffering. The man on the horse is the cancer and all the pain that comes with it. The pain of seeing your wife in pain, of having to take awful medications, of having your life uprooted, of maybe even losing your wife.

It's easy to sympathise with Ahmed and feel that this suffering is inevitable and just what we must deal with as humans before we die a meaningless death. Perhaps we are not as special as we think we are. We are just animals driven by our biological needs to survive and reproduce. But that view is naïve. There *is* a reason for the suffering even if it isn't evident yet.

We all have a snake inside of us that needs suffering to get rid of it. Maybe it's low self-esteem that holds you back from your dreams, or a lack of control over your anger that pushes people away from you, or the snake could be a lack of gratitude that holds you back from living a joyful life and believing you'll only be happy when you have certain things.

I was raised in the Catholic faith and went to church every Sunday. When I met Natasha, it was our mutual faith that helped us connect and keep our relationship strong over time. We would go to church and often perform music together during services. I was on reading rosters and parish councils. My faith was always strong and I had never had any reason to question what my faith meant.

Two years after Natasha was diagnosed, I began to question where God was in our lives. I was furious with God and felt I had every reason to be. Natasha was in so much pain and discomfort from treatment, our lives had been uprooted, we could not have children due to the cancer, and most scans she had showed the cancer spreading. I was losing hope. In my mind, if God was so powerful and loving, then why was this happening? Was God punishing us for something? Was God trying to teach us something? Is there even a God? Was God actually as powerful as we were told? I thought God had abandoned us and left us alone. I didn't know why but possibly I was feeling so alone and confused in general that it made sense that God would also abandon me.

These are questions people of any faith, not only Christians, will most likely feel at some point. They are tough questions because there are so few answers, if any at all. The answers we are given are difficult to comprehend anyway. It's hard to talk about these questions with anyone, especially if you feel isolated already. I could never find the answers I needed and the idea of suffering was too complex for me to understand.

The epiphany I'm about to share will probably not make much sense, but it's possible that at some point during your journey, or even a few years down the track, the lesson might click.

Natasha could understand when I started to talk about my faith struggles with her. She had already been questioning why God had allowed this suffering to happen. She told me God was giving her the strength she needed to carry out her mission in life. She didn't know why her life was ending earlier than expected, but she did know there was nothing she could do about it. She felt strongly that the cancer was God's plan for her, even if it made no sense at all. So, she made a leap of faith to surrender entirely to whatever happened and to be happy in the process. By doing so she was no longer angry with God but instead felt God's strength guiding her and helping her.

I talked to a Catholic monk, who is a good friend, about this and he understood what I meant with Natasha's story. He said Natasha had used the power of God's love to transform her suffering into a joyful experience. Friends who visited us could not believe the strength Natasha had and that she was almost always happy to see them. Natasha told me she always had a choice to be angry and sad about what was happening, or to not let the cancer define who she was and to live a powerful and inspiring life. Natasha believed only God could give her the strength to transform her suffering and to choose how she suffered. The priest told me that on earth we are limited by our bodies. We typically think of love as an emotion or feeling, but that is the only way we can express love through our bodies. When we take away our bodies, nothing is holding us back from loving. When we get rid of the black snake within us, all that's left is joy and possibility.

Towards the end of her life, one of Natasha's oncologists came to see her in the hospital. He told us that he was not a religious person but had seen enough deaths to understand spirituality and what it meant to people. He described death as having everything stripped bare and leaving only love. In death Natasha was indeed stripped of everything material in her life - her job, money, family, and ultimately her body - but it was in this ultimate surrender that her love came through the strongest. There was nothing left to hold her love back.

This might sound strange because if we have lost our bodies then that means we are dead and therefore cannot possibly love. This is where the idea of Heaven comes in. To be in Heaven means to be living for eternity in a dimension we cannot possibly comprehend with the senses we as humans have. This is similar to the concept explored in the film *Interstellar*, in which the character Brand states,

"Maybe it means something more - something we cannot yet understand. Maybe it's some evidence, some artefact of a higher dimension that we cannot consciously perceive. I'm drawn across the universe to someone I haven't seen in a decade, who I know is probably dead. Love is the one thing we're capable of perceiving that transcends dimensions of time and space. Maybe we should trust that, even if we cannot understand it."

Even though Natasha has passed away, I feel her love more powerfully than ever. This was entirely unexpected because I felt her love and I loved her for the eleven years we were together. This is what the monk and oncologist were telling me that when everything is stripped away there is only love left.

You can experience this in some way without dying and this is the most powerful lesson death teaches us. You can choose to feel the love from others and yourself, and to love others. All religions come down to this basic yet difficult lesson: to love others as we hope to be loved. It's difficult though, because people are distracted by the black snakes that hold them back, such as in their pursuit of material things like wealth, power and fame. But if you talk to anyone who is dying, they are quick to point out that these are by far the least important aspects of life and that getting rid of those desires frees us to focus on the important aspects of life. All that matters is how much we loved others and were loved. That love is what will last forever.

This is where God is in this journey of ours. You can channel this love and strength for yourself and for your wife. The loving energy in the universe wants to comfort your wife and tell her she is loved, but the only way this can happen is through your love for her. Your love will transform into the actions of caring for her. Your love will transform into the most intense strength you've ever felt and will get you through sleepless nights and unimaginable pain. Nothing else can do this except love. Even if you aren't religious, you can feel love and you can love. This is all you need to do. God gives us the free will to make this choice but it will be the most powerful choice you can ever make.

I'm now closer to God than I have ever been because I know God is not some man in the sky. God is far more powerful than humans can even comprehend. If God is love and this universal energy, then all of us can experience and share this. That makes more sense to me than any other explanation of God and could only have happened with the suffering of this journey.

It's difficult to share the epiphany I have had, but I hope some of it makes sense to you, even if not entirely right now. Rest assured that no matter how you feel about God right now, God is there waiting for you and is always with you even if you cannot sense that presence. All you need to do, even though this is one of the most difficult choices, is love yourself enough to feel God's love. Love is a gift you don't need to earn, but you must be open to receiving it.

Many people around us with a basic understanding of religion questioned whether Natasha had sinned and was being punished by God. You might have people in your life questioning the same about your wife. Let's be clear in this: God does not punish. The whole idea of God's forgiveness is that no matter what you've done, or failed to do, or thought, God will forgive you and love you unconditionally. None of us can ever be perfect and God does not expect *you* to be perfect. He loves you as you are. So, the idea of punishment for sins is wrong and anyone with a true understanding of God's love will understand this.

Prayer Is Another Concept You Might Struggle With

Gratitude is what helps us to love because we focus on what is abundant in us already rather than what is missing.

When Natasha and I were reflecting on what we were grateful for each day or in our life, we would pray and thank God for these blessings. We would pray for healing as well but we were at peace with whatever happened knowing that there is so much more to life than the time we are in human form. Although Natasha was not physically healed, God did bring us love and gave us the strength to love each other and to love others and to receive love from our friends and families.

Although a part of me wants Natasha to still be here, I know her love was enough. It was an amazing gift but the hardest task of all was to be open to receiving it. For a long time, my heart was closed to receiving her love because I didn't feel God's presence or love. But when my heart was opened eventually, through the epiphany I have described in this chapter, I knew that love was there all along. It's fitting to quote St Paul here, in the words read out at my wedding to Natasha:

"Love is patient, love is kind. It does not envy, it does not boast, it is not proud. It does not dishonour others, it is not self-seeking, it is not easily angered, it keeps no record of wrongs. Love does not delight in evil but rejoices with the truth. It always protects, always trusts, always hopes, always perseveres. Love never fails. And now these three remain: faith, hope and love. But the greatest of these is love. "
– St Paul, in his letter to the Corinthians

Focus on where the love is in your life and you'll realise this is all that ever matters.

Conclusion

*"To live is to change, to be perfect
is to have changed often."*
– Cardinal Henry Newman

Here we are, at the end of this journey through the book together. Your journey with your wife might still be going. If it is, I wish you all the best as you continue. My words will always be here for you. If some advice wasn't applicable when you read it the first time, it might apply at another time. You'll have changed due to this journey you've been on. Whether you've made some plans, or you've shifted your whole mindset and approach, there will have been change. And you will change, as discussed in this final part of the book, by going on the Hero's Journey with your wife.

Change is nothing to be afraid of, even though humans like to be comfortable. Change is inevitable throughout everyone's life, not only for those of us on this journey. You've just had to deal with an extreme version of change, including possibly losing your beloved wife. Even if the worst happens, this change is okay. You *can* get through the change and you *will*.

One of the biggest changes will be within yourself as a man, a husband, a carer, a father, and an employee or employer. You'll have been broken beyond your perceived limits in ways you never imagined yet this is precisely what will strengthen you beyond your previous limits.

Thank you for loving your wife, supporting her, pushing yourself beyond all human limits, and being her protector and defender. Her Hero.

I would love to hear from you, and I reply to every email. james@ jamesgutteridge.com.au

- Your friend, James

Acknowledgements

To Natasha

I don't know if you are reading this but you can anyway feel it in my heart. Thank you for loving me and being patient as I stumbled through our journey together. You taught me and changed me to becoming a whole new man in our 11 years together; to become the man you saw deep down inside that I couldn't even see. Your cancer was painful and arduous, but your never-ending smile, gratitude, strength, faith and love inspired me and always will. Rest in peace knowing that all the lessons I learned from you and our journey are now helping men and couples forever more, or at least until humans eradicate cancer.

To My Mother Carolyn

Mum, thank you for your constant editing of this book. Every time I completed a new edit you would print it off the same day and read it the next. Then a week later I would have a parcel in the letterbox (often including some of your latest baking!) with a thousand edits to go through. Thank you for your thoroughness and belief in the mission. Thank you also for your support as I cared for Natasha. You were always the first one to get on a plane or a call, or send up supplements, or share the latest research. You stepped up even more after Natasha died, and made me realise how lucky I am to still have you around. I wish one piece of advice in the book could have been "Find a mum like mine".

To Lisa

I know it was painful, as my second wife, to read about the journey I had with Natasha, especially its tragedy. You have been an incredible source of encouragement after stepping into my life. You listened and gave feedback as I have thrown ideas around. Your editing has been thorough and ruthless, which is yet another sign of how much you believe in this book's mission. Thank you for it all, for your love, and for standing with me as we bring this book to men all over the world.

To My Editor Samantha

Samantha, you took a haphazard collection of chapters I had written individually and somehow pieced them together into a coherent book. Your advice made me realise that writing my first book was not as simple as punching out a draft in 6 months and hitting print. You have a knack for delivering criticism as compliments, and I would love that skill! Thank you for all your help and believing in this mission.

To My Family And Friends

To all my family and friends who supported me throughout the journey, during and after, thank you. I was afraid to reach out and admit I needed your help, but when I did it came like a waterfall. Whether it was visits, phone calls, packing up my belongings into storage, taking me go-karting, or just making me a meal. I couldn't have gotten through without you. Especially to my sister Morgan for putting up with me living with you, and my grief, after

Natasha died. One of my core pieces of advice in this book is for men to reach out for help too because it probably saved my life.

Thank you to Oliver, Sacha, Adrian and Luwa for your valuable proofreading, and to all the men in my life who provided feedback on the book cover, title and overall strategy. To Pat for your beautiful foreword and for manning up and reaching out as soon as disaster hit. Thank you for your inspiration.

To Natasha's Medical Specialists
I won't mention you by name to protect Natasha, but thank you to every single one of you who cared for Natasha. She lived 3.5 years from her diagnosis, 3 years longer than most doctors thought she should have. I cannot thank you enough for that.

To Inspired Publishing South Africa
Darren, when I first told you about the book idea and my dream for this to help every man caring for a wife with cancer, your excitement was palpable. Thank you for believing in this and putting your hard-working team to work in creating the book covers, the internal design, getting this into bookstores and for the marketing advice.

Mentors and Inspirations
To the medical doctors, social workers and psychologists who provided insight for the book. I won't mention you by name to protect your privacy, but you know who you are. You made this book complete with the very latest medical advice. Any errors that have come through in the book are my own.

Thank you to all the therapists who helped me during my journey and who still are, and to Dr Preeya Alexander my GP in Melbourne for helping me see the light at the end of the tunnel when I couldn't see it. I had no idea that GPs and therapists could help in this way and once I witnessed the miracle work you do, it had to become a central focus of this book.

Thank you to Fr Sacha for your expert spiritual direction after Natasha died, most of all for helping me to forgive and love myself after all the mistakes I made. You are a true friend. Lisa and I were blessed to have you marry us. Thank you also to Dr Draško Dizdar for your spiritual direction and for your beautiful retreat centre Emmaus in Tasmania, where I had the epiphany I shared in the penultimate chapter.

To Brian Johnson for creating Optimize and helping me with membership to your Mastery program after Natasha died. I'm proud to say I'm now an Optimize Coach, and much of the advice in this book has come from your teachings. To Barry Michels and Phil Stutz, creators of *The Tools*, you guys are geniuses and your work is a gift to the world.

Thank you also to my grief counsellors and my fellow widows and widowers in the group for being there with me.

To You The Reader
I cannot stop thanking you for the work you are doing for your wife, often unnoticed. I do not use the words Champion and Hero lightly, and even if you do not feel like either of those things, you are. I never felt like one either because my learning curve just got steeper every day and I was constantly floundering. But you have dedicated yourself to reading this book and to becoming as great a carer and husband you can be. Stand proud.

Further Reading

You can go to the website, www.soyourwifehascancer.com to see a constantly updated list of helpful resources to help you, including links to website and videos.

Websites
- eviQ, accessed from www.eviq.org.au
- Cancer Research UK, accessed from www.cancerresearchuk.org

Books
- Annie Bolitho, *Death: A love project*
- Barry Michels and Phil Stutz: *The tools* and *Coming alive*
- Brandon Bays: *The Journey*
- Carol Dweck, *Mindset: the new psychology of success*
- Dale Carnegie, *How to win friends and influence people*
- David Goggins, *Cannot hurt me*
- David McCullough, *The Wright brothers*
- Eckhart Tolle, *The power of now*
- Elizabeth Dunn and Michael Norton, *Happy money: the new science of smarter spending*
- Gary Chapman, *The 5 Love languages*
- James Nestor, *Breath*
- Jordan Peterson, *12 rules for life*
- Joseph Campbell, *The hero with a thousand faces*
- Martin Seligman, *Learned optimism*
- Matthew Walker, *Why we sleep*
- Miguel Ruiz, *The four agreements*
- Richard Rohr, *Falling upward: a spirituality for the two halves of life*

- Ryan Holiday, *Ego is the enemy*
- Ryan Holiday, *The Obstacle is the way*
- Sheryl Sandberg and Adam Grant, *Option B*
- Simon Sinek, *Start with why*
- Viktor Frankl, *Man's search for meaning*

My Notes

My Notes

My Notes

My Notes

My Notes

My Notes

My Notes

My Notes

My Notes

My Notes

www.ingramcontent.com/pod-product-compliance
Lightning Source LLC
La Vergne TN
LVHW041211080426
835508LV00011B/902